THINKING THE FUTURE

NEW PERSPECTIVES FROM THE SHOULDERS OF GIANTS

CLEM SUNTER & MITCH ILBURY

PENGUIN BOOKS

Thinking the Future
Published by Penguin Books
an imprint of Penguin Random House (Pty) Ltd
Company Reg. No. 1953/000441/07
The Estuaries No. 4, Oxbow Crescent, Century Avenue, Century City, Cape Town, 7441
www.penguinrandomhouse.co.za

Penguin
Random House
South Africa

First published 2021
Reprinted in 2021 (twice) and 2022

5 7 9 10 8 6 4

Publication © Penguin Books 2021
Text © Clem Sunter & Mitch Ilbury

PUBLISHER: Marlene Fryer
MANAGING EDITOR: Ronel Richter-Herbert
EDITOR: Lauren Smith
PROOFREADER: Ronel Richter-Herbert
COVER DESIGN: Sean Robertson
TEXT DESIGN: Ryan Africa
TYPESETTER: Monique van den Berg

Set in 11.5 pt on 15.5 pt Minion

Printed by **novus print**, a division of Novus Holdings

ISBN 978 1 77609 629 9 (print)
ISBN 978 1 77609 630 5 (ePub)

Contents

Contents

This book is dedicated to the giants to come, upon whose shoulders others will stand to unwrap the mysteries of the future.

Acknowledgements

It is unusual for authors to write a book during a pandemic. Covid-19 has meant that we have done all the writing in our respective homes, while remotely communicating with one another and with everybody else involved in the production of the book. In the last regard, we would like to thank Ronel Richter-Herbert who, as managing editor of Penguin Non-fiction in South Africa, has kept the project on track. We would also like to thank Lauren Smith for her editing of our book. All in all, it was an uplifting experience in the most challenging of times.

Chapter 1

May the Fox Be with You

To understand is to perceive patterns.
Isaiah Berlin

Every book has a mission. Ours is to draw on the wisdom of giants, past and present, to help you think more effectively about the future. In the process, we hope you will make better decisions affecting your own and other people's lives. Along the way, we'll offer some of our own opinions on the future too.

As Isaiah Berlin noted in the quote above, the capacity to recognise patterns plays a prominent role in our understanding of the things around us. For that reason, we'll start our lesson in thinking the future by taking a close look at a famous picture about two ways of perceiving the world.

Making Sense of the World

In the centre of one of the world's most beautiful paintings lies a secret hidden in plain sight. Raphael's *School of Athens* (1509–1511) – a hallmark of the Italian Renaissance – imagines an idyllic scene where ancient Greece's most iconic thinkers are engaged in deep reflection and intense debate. At the heart of the painting, framed by four archways that focus the eye, stand two giants of philosophy: Plato and Aristotle. They are the only two figures cast within the light of the blue sky outside. It is their hands that hold the secret.

Plato is pointing up towards the heavens, symbolising his theory of forms – a belief that everything we see in our physical world is simply a 'copy' of an ideal form that exists in a different realm. Aristotle, although a student of Plato, saw things differently. His hand is held out towards the viewer, turned down as if to suggest that we must take our cue not from some mysterious realm, but from that which appears grounded in reality – our *experience* of the world.

Plato's theory was ambitious. He searched for the true *essence* of things – the blueprint for our world. His philosophy was about trying to understand the ideal forms of things and seeing them in their true light, which the allegory now famously known as Plato's Cave tries to explain. Imagine yourself deep down in a cave, shackled to a chair, staring at a wall. You've been looking at this wall all your life and are unable to turn your head around. Behind you is a fire, in front of which people are carrying an assortment of puppets and figurines based on real things in the world outside the cave. The light of the fire casts shadows of the puppets and figurines on the wall in front of you, but you can't see the objects themselves.

For Plato, basing our understanding of the world on our experiences alone would be akin to chasing the shadows on the wall. Philosophy, for him, was about emerging from the cave to see the real world in the true light of the sun. This theory shaped his view on all things.

Aristotle, on the other hand, thought like a scientist: that we should be rooted in experience and work our way up. He examined the available evidence and structured a logical argument to try to explain what might be happening. He saw no evidence that life on earth was full of shadows. He wanted to look at things closely and try to understand them for what they were.

It is a mark of Raphael's mastery that, in two simple hand gestures, he manages to capture a fundamental distinction between the philosophical approaches of two of history's greatest thinkers, and how we as humans have used both approaches to try to make sense of the world.

We can learn a lot by comparing the thinking of these two architects of Western philosophy. The key distinction lies in the size of their bets. Plato's approach was guided by one overarching theory. Get it right and everything clicks into place like a giant jigsaw puzzle. Get it wrong, though, and you'll be squishing down mismatched pieces until the futility becomes so clear that sweeping the puzzle off the table in frustration is the only option. This is because Plato's approach presupposes that only a privileged few – an elite club of deep-thinking philosophers who emerge from the cave to see the real world – have access to the puzzle box. Only they can see the big picture that then guides their thinking on which piece goes where.

Aristotle's approach doesn't depend on being able to see the box. His method of inquiry isn't guided by an overarching theory of how things *should* fit together. Rather, his approach points to the fact that we can still piece together a coherent picture without a preconceived image in our head. By analysing each piece and methodically connecting the component parts, we can assemble a valid and compelling view of reality.

At this juncture you may be wondering what the reasoning of philosophers from thousands of years ago has to do with thinking the future. Before we answer that, it would be prudent to outline what it means to 'think the future'.

What Is 'Thinking the Future'?

Every decision we make relates to the future in some way. Whether it be the subject choice of a child in school; when and where a family decides to move home; how a business maps out strategic decisions for future profits; or the way a government goes about fiscal policymaking to address a looming debt burden: decisions made in the present are shaped by what we believe or hope the future holds. To this extent, the deliberations of today are intimately tied to our thoughts of tomorrow.

The thing is, thinking the future can be done well, or it can be done poorly. Because of its importance in our decision-making, falling on the wrong side of this divide can have marked consequences. The subjects you learn at school, the neighbourhood you live in or the fiscal policies that a government implements will all affect the experiences you have after those decisions are made and, in the worst-case scenario, those experiences can prove to be tragic. Thus, thinking the future has a make-or-break element to it that lies in the quality of the decisions we take.

This prompts the question: How do you know if you're thinking the future *well*? You may think the answer is simple: Accuracy. Surely your futures thinking is effective if your vision turns out to be an accurate prediction of what plays out in reality? Undoubtedly, accuracy is important – if it was not part of the answer, then all estimates for how the future may play out would have equal value. It wouldn't matter if you were right or wrong and there would be no accountability – no yardstick for success. But assuming that it's *just* about accuracy is misleading.

Focusing on accuracy leads to three problems. First, we tend to home in on more precise estimates than the uncertainty of the situation allows, which means failing to account for the complexity and unpredictability of the world. Second, it leads to the assumption that we should bet big on *one single answer*, when it would be wiser to prepare for multiple eventualities. And third, it puts all the emphasis on the *outcome* of the prediction, when the *process* underpinning it is of equal importance. You might guess the future out of pure luck or intuition, but that doesn't necessarily teach you anything about how to make decisions. Conversely, you may have followed a robust process that turns out to be wrong simply because life is unpredictable, but the method itself and the information gathered will reveal something useful about the patterns at play. So, accuracy is part of the answer, but not all of it.

The essence of thinking the future is to understand the pattern of forces propelling the present into the future and to see where those forces can lead. It is about posing the right questions to help you detect the changes in the game in which you are a participant, whether it's related to where you live, the occupation you are in or the interests that you have. It can extend to global issues like climate change, but it can also be about the societal trends in your own country or community that are bringing people together or driving them apart. It can be about technology and what industries are becoming obsolete or more relevant. At present, it is very much about how the nature of work, private life and education will be altered by the coronavirus pandemic and economic lockdowns.

It is also about coming to terms with certain facts of life that won't change in the foreseeable future, which we can use to rule out scenarios that contradict those facts. For example, humans won't be migrating to another planet if this one becomes uninhabitable, at least not in the near future, so we need to focus on how to keep living here and not continue behaving as if we have other options.

Once you've figured out the pattern of forces shaping the future you're interested in, the next step is to see where those forces might lead. This can take various forms, one of which is forecasting. This type of futures thinking follows the existing pattern of information along a single line of projection to provide one prediction. The weather report is perhaps the most common example. However, this singular, right-or-wrong approach has its pitfalls, and our preferred technique is scenario planning, where you use the pattern of forces to plot out a plausible narrative, or set of narratives, about what could happen in the next year, decade or century – whatever the time period you've selected.

You can only do this by consulting your experience of the real world around you and envisaging the possible chains of cause and effect that lie within the realms of reason. This is why we favour the Aristotelian approach as opposed to that recommended by Plato: having a preconceived notion of the future based on an ideal world does not help in this regard. Your hopes may be dashed by an unexpected turn of events that could not be captured by pure introspection.

Putting an emphasis on experience and reason does not mean that the future will look like a logical continuation of the past. Such extrapolation can be just as dangerous. Indeed, we all know that this century is already like no previous one because of advances in technology and the planet being home to a record number of human beings. The challenge is to see where these factors will lead, along with any other forces identified. Imagination is a helpful assistant in the task of thinking the future creatively and seeing how it can differ from the past. That said, too much imagination and not enough logic can lead to wild speculation that's not grounded in reality. Reason and imagination must go hand in hand.

Finally, we must dispel the notion that thinking the future only applies to long periods of time. Futurists, like prophets, are considered by many to be an exclusive cadre with a rare talent or skill for gazing into the distant unknown. We are writing this book so that our readers can look at something important next week, next year, or even in five to ten years' time and make a more careful and informed decision about it. Uncertainty grows the further you look ahead, but even the next twenty-four hours can contain a surprise.

Obviously, you sometimes need to balance the short-term against the long-term future, in which case you must ensure that the narratives you compose for both do not contradict one another. For example, planning a whole set of overseas trips next year will inevitably increase your carbon footprint, which may conflict with your long-term scenario that humankind must work together to ensure that your children have a sustainable future.

Having defined what we mean by thinking the future, we would like to develop another duality that reveals our preference for flexibility over rigidity. However, even though the idea also originates in ancient Greece, we must fast-forward 450 years from Raphael's Rome to twentieth-century Oxford and a philosophical giant in his own right: Professor Isaiah Berlin. He put the duality on the map.

Foxes and Hedgehogs

In his famous essay 'The Hedgehog and The Fox', Isaiah Berlin unearths a seemingly simple line from the ancient Greek poet Archilochus: 'The fox knows many things, but the hedgehog knows one big thing.'

Berlin cultivated this small shoot into a wider analogy and used it to distinguish the philosophical bent of some of history's greatest thinkers. Some, he said, were singular in their thinking, relating everything to one big idea. They constructed an all-encompassing theory and saw the world according to that theory. In this sense, they were hedgehogs. Others were more diffuse in their thinking and operated on multiple levels. Through experience, they saw things for what they were in themselves without seeking to fit them into, or exclude them from, any one unitary inner vision. They were foxes.

Berlin considered the likes of Dante, Lucretius, Proust and Nietzsche classic hedgehogs, and thinkers such as Herodotus, Montaigne, Goethe and Joyce typical foxes. Modern-day examples may include Ronald Reagan, Barack Obama, Adrian Gore and Angela Merkel as foxes: they've seen things from different perspectives and have managed to balance competing views to arrive at innovative solutions. On the other hand, Lee Kuan Yew, Margaret Thatcher, Jeremy Corbyn and Donald Trump could be considered hedgehogs: for better or for worse, their thinking has been guided by a stubborn, singular focus. If Berlin were gazing at Raphael's *School of Athens*, he'd point to Plato and say 'hedgehog', leaving Aristotle as the fox.

Although not designed to be a rigid classification, the hedgehog–fox analogy fits what Raphael captured in his illustrative distinction between Plato and Aristotle. Hedgehogs try to find simplicity in the complex – a unifying thread that ties everything together. Foxes are more comfortable with complexity. They don't risk pushing down too hard on the puzzle pieces so as to force them into a predetermined shape. Instead, they assess each piece and allow for the possibility that it might change the pattern and the picture as a whole.

Berlin himself was a fox too, or at least anti-hedgehog. He declared, in 'Notes on Prejudice':

> Few things have done more harm than the belief on the part of individuals or groups (or tribes or states or nations or churches) that he or she or they are in *sole* possession of the truth: especially about how to live, what to be and do – and that those who differ from them are not merely mistaken, but wicked or mad: and need restraining or suppressing. It is a terrible and dangerous arrogance to believe that you alone are right: have a magical eye which sees *the* truth: and others cannot be right if they disagree.

Berlin even included William Shakespeare in his list of foxes and quoted a line from Hamlet's lips to justify his categorisation of the bard: 'There are more things in heaven and earth, Horatio, than are dreamt of in your philosophy.'

So, what does this all mean for thinking the future? Well, how we make sense of the world informs how we think it will unfold. If you're a hedgehog, you're going to lean towards one unifying theory to explain a causal chain of events. For example, an economist relying purely on classical economics to forecast future trends is going to operate on the assumption that individuals function as rational actors. While this undoubtedly simplifies things, it doesn't capture the full picture, and misrepresents reality in the name of a preconceived puzzle-box picture.

If you're a fox, you'll be more open to different explanations for how things may turn out. The foxy economist knows that humans are not always rational and will therefore look to other theories in behavioural economics to counterbalance classical projections. For example, nudging consumers to buy particular items in shops by putting them close to the till is a recognised tactic for increasing demand. It goes against the principle in classical economic theory that the *only* way to boost demand is to lower the price of the product. Foxy economists will have a more nuanced perspective, appreciating the range of possible behaviours, both rational and irrational, that one can expect from consumers. As such, their understanding will be closer to reality.

On the surface, foxes may look like they're complicating things but, in reality, they're attempting to refine their understanding by seeing things from different perspectives. In a well-trodden, somewhat predictable environment, the hedgehog reigns supreme. In the more complicated, uncertain environments that make up most of the world, where a new normal is often completely different to the old one, the fox has the flexibility to survive and thrive.

Good, But Not Great

So, are foxes superior to hedgehogs? You might not think so if you listened to Jim Collins. You may have his book *Good to Great* (2001) on your shelf, perhaps wedged between your copies of *Rich Dad Poor Dad* and *Who Moved My Cheese?* It was one of those business books that caused quite a buzz, selling millions of copies in the process.

In the book, Collins claims that you can transform yourself and your organisation from good to great by consistently following 'The Hedgehog Concept'. He suggests that, driven by the determined singular mindset of a hedgehog nature, great leaders build companies around a crystalline concept that defines what those companies are about. This Hedgehog Concept is made up of three parts: firstly, what you are deeply passionate about; secondly, what you can be the best in the world at; and thirdly, what drives your economic engine. Identifying these things honestly, and consistently applying the resultant clarity of purpose, is the key to your success.

Collins makes some good points. Clarity of purpose is important for effective leadership and implementation of strategy. Identifying what your business can be exceptional at will probably help establish a distinctive competency. Moreover, being a hedgehog by nature is nothing to scoff at. Some of the most legendary athletes, businesspeople and activists attribute their success to a singular vision of their future, and their relentless drive towards an ambitious goal. This mentality has become a fetish in motivational teachings. The young and ambitious are told that if they mould a dream rigidly around an activity they are good at and forge on without relenting – just like Michael Jordan, Tiger Woods, Yo-Yo Ma and Serena Williams – they, too, can reach stardom.

There is nothing wrong with giving young people drive and ambition by providing inspirational figures, but it has to be admitted that the exceptional are just that: exceptional. Moreover, the argument frequently equates the pursuit of happiness with the pursuit of profit. Certainly, focus counts in the case of a company, and being too much of a conglomerate in the corporate world is now seen as a recipe for financial mediocrity, or even ruin. However, the principle of hedgehog-like focus cannot simply be transferred from business to society in general. There is something to be said for versatility in the lives of ordinary people and for having a variety of pastimes and other interests. Hence the adage that variety is the spice of life.

Furthermore, suggesting that success is achievable purely through effective *internal* organisation around a central belief can blindside us, in that we will not give enough attention to a changing *external* environment. World heavyweight boxing champion Mike Tyson puts it more bluntly: 'Everyone has a plan until they get punched in the mouth.' In his own way, Tyson alludes to what evolution teaches us: sustainable success depends on the ongoing adaptation of internal strategies to evolving external circumstances. In the ringside analogy, the best foxes will reflect on their bobbing and weaving and post-punch bloody-mouth moments just as much as their winning hook-jab-uppercut combinations. When they fail, they learn from it and revise their approach. Hedgehogs would stick to the strategy they already know and simply try to go in harder, no matter whom or what they're going up against.

Let's look at foxy thinking in a more relatable example: a young professional wanting to own her first home in five years' time. She can calculate what she needs to save each month to be able to put down a deposit, and she can determine the size of the bond she needs to buy a place in her dream location. Focused on what she wants and what she needs to do to get it, she's well placed to pursue her goal like a hedgehog. But she would be remiss if she does not adopt a foxy approach by also monitoring external forces, such as the state of the economy, fluctuations in the property market, the security and viability of the business she works for, and the changing trends in the way people work.

All these factors could influence when, where and even if she can buy property in five years. She may need to change jobs for higher pay, make tougher lifestyle choices to save more and look for locations with better prices. Even then, she might, in five years, decide to use the savings to start her own business. Foxes are equally as ambitious as hedgehogs, but they're more aware of the potential need to adapt and revise their plans if circumstances change. And they can accept that even the best-laid plans go awry.

Thinking the future like a hedgehog, on the other hand, tends to inflate our inner belief that we can shape our own future *irrespective of external influence*. That's very alluring – we want to believe we are the masters of our own destiny. But too much hot air and an inflated belief in ourselves make us increasingly susceptible to life's rough edges and sharp corners. Of course, the unrelenting pursuit of one goal may get us through some tough times. We achieve a certain measure of resilience by facing adversity and recognising our personal shortcomings. The problem arrives when you repeat the same mistakes over and over again because your hedgehoggy self-belief insists that you have the power to make your plan work no matter what. If you're a fox, you'll adapt and change. And if the dream goes pop and the party ends, you may have other pursuits in mind because you didn't hang all your hopes on one venture. In the long run, you may cope better.

Isaiah Berlin's hedgehog–fox duality was also taken up by Philip Tetlock – a professor of psychology at the Wharton School, University of Pennsylvania. His 2005 book *Expert Political Judgement: How Good Is It? How Can We Know?* was a seminal study on the ability of experts to forecast the future along a single line. Spoiler alert – they're not very good. In fact, they're so bad that Tetlock says we might as well trust our predictions to dart-throwing chimpanzees. And he studied over 82 000 forecasts over two decades to reach this conclusion.

Tetlock didn't just embarrass experts; he embarrassed hedgehogs too. He used Berlin's analogy as a categorical distinction between differing approaches to forecasting the future. Generally, experts and hedgehogs share an inner confidence in their ability to predict outcomes on a given line of enquiry. Years of rigorous study and experience within a particular field have meant experts are labelled as such because of their firm grasp of the subject in question. To quote Archilochus, 'they know one big thing'.

In almost every major news source you will find a collection of political journalists, and former special advisers, who are steeped in historical knowledge in all things political. They're a special breed of political junkie that loves to watch, analyse and commentate on the ins and outs of the revolving door that is political life. Logic suggests that this should put them in a great position to, say, assess the likelihood of a given candidate winning an upcoming election.

The counterargument is that their expertise actually puts them at a disadvantage when thinking the future. They're so schooled in the way things *have been*, and the way things *are*, that they dismiss ideas of the way things *may turn out*. They expand conventional theories to explain new and emerging cases that don't necessarily fit the mould. With highly tuned ears, they listen out for specific cues that signal the tropes with which they are familiar. But their well-grooved experience means that they're more likely to dismiss evidence that would play a different tune. Hedgehogs have a limited playlist.

In 2016, Donald Trump exposed the limited playlist of political pundits the world over. How could someone who breaks so many of the written and unwritten rules of political campaigning be elected to hold the highest office in America? In the lead-up to the election, liberal news sources were replete with flabbergasted political commentators speculating that Trump's moment in the sun was a flash in the pan. These well-grooved thinkers had a persistent confidence in the belief that Democrat front-runner Hillary Clinton would triumph. When the votes were counted, how wrong they were.

They'd failed to see the potential for an upset, despite the signs of growing anti-establishment sentiment, driven by the pervasive spread of misinformation. These signs were all around them, and yet a Trump presidency was unthinkable in light of how things had always been – at least from their perspective. They'd argued that no one could say the things Trump said and get away with it. Their excuse now would be that they were only wrong by four years and sanity has returned with Joe Biden's victory in 2020!

Berlin would have rated most writers of opinion pieces in today's newspapers as hedgehogs in that they reflect the conservative or liberal ethos of the newspaper to which they regularly contribute. For example, the emergency relief measures taken by governments to combat the economic fallout from the coronavirus pandemic are represented in some conservative media articles as a recipe for a major uptick in inflation in the years ahead. Too much money will be chasing too few goods. Buy gold or cryptocurrencies now.

On the other hand, writers for the liberal press present the view that the only way to recover quickly from the lockdown is for governments to proceed with major relief packages immediately. The inflation rate will not rise significantly, and the global economic turnaround will arrive sooner. You, as the reader, must assess the plausibility of the futures portrayed, and that requires the judgement of a fox. As Jemima Kelly, a shrewd columnist for the *Financial Times*, observed in an article in January 2021: 'We live in a world that rewards those who speak with conviction – even when that is misplaced – and give very little time to those that acknowledge doubt.'

We do need experts – they're a rich source of deep knowledge on subject matters we can't all hope to master, but we should never forget that they don't necessarily have a firmer grasp on the future than we do. A more honed perspective, definitely, but they should serve as a resource we *refer* to, not *defer* to.

The Power of the Fox

Tetlock's study was influential not only because it shone a light on why hedgehogs make such poor forecasters, but also why foxes make such good ones. He points out that foxes consistently edge out hedgehogs in regional forecasting studies, and the more complex reasoning process they go through sheds light on their winning streak:

The foxes' self-critical, point-counterpoint style of thinking prevented them from building up the sorts of excessive enthusiasm for their predictions that hedgehogs, especially well-informed ones, displayed for theirs.

Simply put, foxes question their assumptions. Not in some superficial way just for the sake of argument; instead, they incorporate critical doubt as an essential element in their methodological approach. Instead of seeing doubt as a threat to their ability to explain the world around them, they see doubt as an opportunity to improve it. Through doubt, they can balance perspectives, test multiple theories, expose fault lines in their reasoning and revise their assumptions in the face of new evidence. If you think that sounds Aristotelian, you would be right. And it seems simple because it is. Healthy doubt is also the principle that guides robust science and structures rational thinking. So why, we ask, wouldn't it also underpin the futures thinking done by experts?

Alas, Tetlock's story takes us only so far. As definitive as his study was in refining the science of prediction, it didn't exactly dial back the hubris among forecasters. The one thing potentially more dangerous than consistently getting predictions wrong is consistently getting them right: it buoys the belief that success breeds success. Normally this can be exhilarating, but in futures thinking success can breed overconfidence. Every prediction we get right grows the confidence in our ability to get the next one right. If forecasting were purely an academic exercise, a matter of researchers trading chest bumps, that would be fine. But when predictions inform critical decisions that affect our lives, then excessive confidence is kryptonite to good futures thinking for everyone.

It is ironic that accurate predictions increase our reliance on them. The outcome, unfortunately, is a misguided sense of confidence to increase a bet until things go spectacularly wrong – like a gambler on a winning streak at roulette choosing to put everything on a specific number. Alas, it does not come up with the next spin of the wheel. Every valuable forecast is entirely dependent on asking the right questions. Track record does not count.

Pierre Wack, the 'superstar' of scenario planning at Royal Dutch Shell, and a featured giant in Chapter 4, equated forecasting, with its narrow focus, to shining a torch into a dim room for a brief moment. That glimpse may be useful in terms of giving you a clearer insight as to what's there. But it becomes folly to build a longer-term picture from that one image if everyone inside the room is playing musical chairs in the semi-darkness. Just when you think you know what's what and who's where, the music starts, the contents of the room spin, and you have to reshine your light, this time showing a totally different configuration.

Forecasting is a bit like *Storage Wars*, an American reality TV show about auctioning off storage lockers where the owners have stopped paying rent. Professional buyers are given five minutes to assess the contents without stepping inside the locker or touching any of the items. The buyers may initially get excited when seeing jet-ski handlebars poking out from behind a large box, only to win the bid and find out that they're not actually connected to a jet-ski.

Just like forecasters, the bidders have to imagine what could be in the locker based on very little evidence. The limited view means they have to extrapolate small indicators into larger stories. Some buyers make money across the season after averaging out their winnings and losses. More often than not, however, those same successful buyers let their perceived ability go to their heads and throw away all their profits on the next big bet, which turns out to be a whole lotta' nothing.

Foxes Don't Forecast

To mitigate the risk of relying on forecasts, Tetlock believed that the forecasters should qualify them by assigning each one with a probability of turning out to be correct, based on statistical data gathered from the past. In doing so, he allowed for the possibility that the forecast need not come true. However, we would go further by saying that true foxes wouldn't admit to being forecasters at all. They're too smart for that. How foxes make sense of the world is antithetical to the idea that we have any kind of firm grasp on how it will play out. Now this doesn't mean that they just sit back and sip tea, waiting for life to happen to them. Rather, they entertain different theories for how the future will unfold, and don't narrow their focus down to a detailed projection of just one. They imagine multiple possible futures. Foxes, at their very core, are scenario planners.

This idea of linking foxes to futures thinking was first introduced to the world by one of the authors of this book, Clem Sunter, when he connected the dots from standing on the shoulders of two giants of his past. Clem crossed paths with Isaiah Berlin while reading politics, philosophy and economics at Oxford University in the 1960s. Then, in the mid-1980s, he worked closely with Pierre Wack and the teams assembled by the Anglo American Corporation in London and Johannesburg, to craft scenarios for the world and South Africa in the 1990s.

In 1999, in his book *Never Mind the Millennium. What about the next 24 hours?*, Clem wrote the following:

> Foxes take after quantum physicists who accept that the future is driven by the principle of uncertainty, and there'll always be things we don't know and can't control ... they regularly take bites out of the 'reality sandwich' to keep their feet on the ground. They therefore have a healthy scepticism of grand visions which portray the world as a highly mechanistic and predictable system.

It wasn't until the following year, when he met Chantell Ilbury – a successful entrepreneur – that the idea of inventing a practical tool to translate Berlin's analogy into thinking about the future took shape. Clem had already been using his presentations to demonstrate to numerous audiences that scenario planning could become a popular discipline and should not remain the preserve of governments and multinational corporations. He and Chantell agreed that all institutions, large and small, as well as individuals thinking about the future for themselves and their families, should be exposed to the methodology.

The melding of their thinking produced *The Mind of a Fox* – a bestselling book published in June 2001. Apart from offering a model for foxes to follow, the two authors jointly wanted to combat hedgehog thinkers who were deeply committed to one projection of the future, consistent with their preferred way of viewing the world. This type of approach was evident in many boardrooms around the world, where business strategies were rigidly based on the directors' own interpretation of the company's vision, mission statement and objectives – take it or leave it. Questions about changes in the commercial environment that might undermine the chosen strategy were either dismissed as frivolous or treated as an afterthought. The risks were never properly evaluated.

The book contained a hypothetical letter to George Bush, offering him one prospective event and two global scenarios to ponder in order to persuade him to start thinking like a fox as US president:

> Yet another consequence of being one family multiplying on one Earth is the growing possibility of worldwide epidemics … You cannot have healthy economies with sick people. With urbanization, migration and the mutation of bacteria and viruses into drug-resistant forms, an old-fashioned plague of some kind which will affect everyone is looming large; and the doctors' arsenal of antibiotics is looking desperately thin.

Their letter goes on to say:

> We'll sketch two mainframe scenarios which for convenience are named 'Friendly Planet' and 'Gilded Cage'. In Friendly Planet the rich old millions resolve to find common ground with the poor young billions to eradicate poverty and disease, to tackle problems of the environment, to bring international criminal syndicates to justice and to root out dangerous terrorist organisations. All nations jointly agree to solve any problems which are a threat to world peace.
>
> It sounds terribly utopian, but the alternative for the rich old millions is to hole themselves up in a Gilded Cage. That cage can be blown to smithereens at any moment by nuclear-armed terrorists or be gradually overwhelmed by millions of illegal immigrants slipping through the bars to escape anarchy elsewhere. The law of entropy will prevail as nations descend to a common low.

Shortly after these words were written, the world was shaken by the 9/11 terrorist attacks. More recently, we have experienced the coronavirus pandemic and the fairly disappointing lack of coordination in international response to it. We have seen the growing economic inequalities between and within nations stirring up indignation everywhere. Meanwhile, the borders of many developed countries have been more strongly fortified to stop any further influx of migrants from the developing world. One wonders which of the two scenarios the current world leaders would say is in play right now, and what action must be taken to increase the chances of a friendlier planet by 2030.

Among a limited number of somewhat predictable phenomena, there are many variables that can intersect to drive wildly different causal chains. Foxes are best placed to see this. Nevertheless, thinking the future is daunting, even for foxes. There is so much complexity and uncertainty in the path that it can be hard to find a foothold. But our guiding principles are simpler than you might otherwise think.

The underpinning of good futures thinking is simply *good thinking*. It was Isaac Newton who said: 'If I have seen further than others, it is by standing upon the shoulders of giants.' As mentioned at the very beginning, this book looks to the past in order to think the future by standing on the shoulders of some of history's greatest thinkers. From them we have gathered fundamental principles that will help *you* think the future. You can use them individually or collectively to spread your wings and consider positive and negative futures – and find ways to help make the positive ones a reality. The principles can be applied to thinking about the world at large, or to exploring possibilities in your personal life. If Newton can do it, you can do it too.

Being foxes, though, we will never suggest that our interpretation of their wisdom is the *only* one to follow. After all, foxes are modest, knowing that their judgements may be adjusted by obtaining alternative points of view. Perhaps you will come up with an even better set of recommendations after reading this book. Isaiah Berlin, the giant whom we showcased in this opening chapter, has appropriately set the scene for the adventure that lies ahead. May the fox be with you in experiencing it.

Before we move on, however, we would like to ask you some questions to put you into an active frame of mind in thinking the future. We will go through this process at the end of every chapter. You can answer each question after a bout of introspection and chin-stroking, or you can discuss it with friends, relatives and colleagues to get their takes. The questions are a combination of personal and big-picture stuff because we want to highlight the interaction between the observer and observed.

Although the future has, by definition, not yet been experienced by our senses, keen perception and mental acumen enable us to construct plausible ideas of what it holds in store. We can sift through the evidence accumulated in the past and available today to make conjectures about tomorrow. In doing so, being aware of your internal state of mind – particularly your hopes and fears, likes and dislikes – is as essential as being aware of what is happening in the external world. Looking in and looking out in an objective way are equally desirable skills for anybody with the ambitions of a futurist.

As Sun Tzu – an ancient Chinese military strategist – said in *The Art of War*, published in roughly the 5th century BCE:

> If you know the enemy and know yourself, you need not fear the result of a hundred battles. If you know yourself but not the enemy, for every victory gained you will suffer defeat. If you know neither the enemy nor yourself, you will succumb in every battle.

If you view the external environment as the 'enemy' in this analogy, and the battles as scenarios, then Sun Tzu's philosophy can illuminate the practice of futures thinking. If you have a deep understanding of yourself while also being knowledgeable about the world around you, then you will have the capacity to imagine a hundred valuable future scenarios.

The questions are as follows:

1. Would you describe yourself as a hedgehog or a fox? Or are you a bit of both – a hedgefox – depending on the circumstances under which you are peering into the future? In other words, how often do you base your decisions on a single projection of the future that you get either right or wrong, and how often do you keep an open mind and prepare for multiple eventualities?
2. What is the most spectacular future that you got right, and was it a

likely or unlikely one to happen? Did you play any role in making it happen or was it just fate? Perhaps a combination of both?

3. On the other hand, what was the most spectacular future you got wrong and, in retrospect, were there signs you ignored that might have made you more aware of what was actually about to happen?

4. Choose a long-term goal that is important to you. What are the external factors affecting the possibility that you will or will not achieve your goal? If you tend to see the world in simple or straightforward terms, try asking a friend about what factors they see in relation to your goal. It can introduce you to ideas that you've never considered before.

5. Do you think there are certain aspects of humanity and society that will never change and that lend some truth to the old French saying: *plus ça change, plus c'est la même chose* (the more things change, the more they stay the same)? Or is the future never ever what it used to be?

Chapter 2

Questioning Your Assumptions

One thing only I know, and that is that I know nothing.
Socrates

The words above may sound so extreme that you might consider Socrates – the ancient Greek philosopher and featured giant of this chapter – to be a hedgehog hiding under a cloak of humility. In contrast, his assumed ignorance offers an effective counterweight to the false notion that knowledge can be perfect at any point in time. For example, while we are confident that night will continue to follow day as the earth rotates, our knowledge of the universe is continuously being expanded by discoveries such as Einstein's laws of relativity, neutrinos and black holes. There are no absolute truths in the world of perception. Yes, $2 + 2 = 4$ will be true for all time, but that is prescribed by the laws of mathematics, which is a closed system. The universe is an open system, and that applies to all the bodies that exist in it.

Socrates chose to get this message across as his lifetime mission: everything can be questioned because nothing is beyond question. It is well illustrated by something else he said: 'Education is the kindling of a flame, not the filling of a vessel.' One cannot fill a vessel with information and thereby achieve complete understanding. There will always be questions to be asked, illumination to seek.

Nevertheless, before exploring the value of Socrates's legacy when thinking the future, we would like to continue our discussion of the limitations of forecasting, since it assumes a level of knowledge we seldom possess.

Searching for the Black Cat

There's an old philosophical quip that goes like this:

> Philosophy is like a blind man stumbling around a dark cave, looking for a black cat.
>
> Metaphysics is like a blind man stumbling around a dark cave, looking for a black cat that isn't there.
>
> Theology is like a blind man stumbling around a dark cave, looking for a black cat that isn't there, and then shouting: 'I found it!'

Anyone who has grappled with life's biggest questions knows that this joke contains some truth. It's tough to reflect honestly on major philosophical problems and come away from the experience cat-in-hand. But the problem isn't unique to philosophy. We experience a similar feeling when thinking the future: faced with complexity and uncertainty, it's not easy for any of us to find a foothold, let alone a black cat.

In addition, the quip highlights the fact that there are different ways to deal with the angst associated with uncertainty – one more honest than the other. Faced with the unseen territory of the future, and the uncertainty and complexity of all the factors affecting it, you might be tempted to grab onto whatever you find, or even what you simply wish was there. Professional forecasters attempt to deal with uncertainty by constructing manual models or computer algorithms to eliminate it as far as possible.

The models represent a set of pre-defined rules that govern the forces or variables driving the system into the future. Underlying these rules is a set of assumptions. For example, 'when x happens, y happens'. Each one of these assumptions is usually based on past trends and probabilities revealed by statistical analyses. That way, forecasters can point to a track record of what specific variables *tend* to do under certain conditions – like, if you will, the influence of the wind on the trajectory of an arrow or bullet. All that is needed to become a sharpshooting forecaster is to extrapolate the data and aim it at the target with these factors in mind. You may miss, but you will be closer than those who are just guessing.

This approach to dealing with uncertainty has its moments, because there are some aspects of life that unfold in a fairly predictable fashion.

Population growth is a good example. Forecasters are well placed to cap-ture future demographic trends, as it is a widespread assumption that the rate of birth will continue to exceed the rate of death of our species for the foreseeable future. Across the decades we can aggregate the number of people into an ascending population highway, as long as it is wide enough to include a margin of error. Even on this topic, though, you can't take the trends for granted. The UN has recently done a range of population scenarios up to 2100. Due to falling fertility rates, the rising age profile of many nations, climate change and the chances of more pandemics, they don't want to bet on a precise figure. Their median forecast is a total of 10.9 billion people, but there could be various forks in the road ahead.

Moreover, the accuracy of forecasting is inversely proportional to the complexity of the system within which it operates. That is because the more complex the system, the greater the scope of the moving parts. You're going to find it more difficult to wrestle with an octopus than a sea cucumber.

Having said that, it's difficult to formulate any *meaningful* question about the future that is simple enough for a forecast, even with limited moving parts. The world of sport is a great example of this. A game of soccer is only ninety minutes long, with a clearly defined set of rules, a limited number of players and a single ball. It's a relatively simple system, but the distinction between winner and loser often comes down to a matter of inches: a close offside call, a ball hitting the crossbar or a slide tackle in the penalty box gone wrong. You can only know the final score when the final whistle blows.

In the game of life, small moments can have big consequences too, and any meaningful prediction is vulnerable to small variations in the external environment. Put another way, life will always have the potential to make or break your prediction no matter how well thought out it is.

In a 1973 report prepared for the Defense Advanced Research Project Agency (DARPA) – a research agency of the United States Department of Defense, responsible for emerging technologies – Herman Weil and Michael Leavitt point to the extent to which forecasting relies on assumptions:

> Any qualitative or quantitative forecast, either of the short- or long-range
> variety, rests fundamentally upon the assumptions of the forecasting

model utilized. The forecasts themselves can only be valid to the extent that the assumptions of the forecasting model are accurate reflections of the nature of processes in the real world.

In a nutshell, forecasters are only as good as their models. So, when forecasters think about the future, they should ask themselves the following question: Have I accurately captured *all* of the moving parts that can affect change? The people who use forecasts to inform their decision-making need to ask a similar question, but with a different focal point of accountability: How confident am I that this forecast accurately captures all of the moving parts that can affect change?

If a forecast gets through these questions unscathed, then there's one last challenge to overcome: How valuable is it? Leavitt points to the paradoxical relationship between general reliability and specific value when forecasting in international relations:

> For many planning purposes, knowing what is likely to happen is of some interest, but of greater import is knowing what low-probability (but high-cost or high-benefit) situations might be possible. Models that are developed to fit the former criteria will be hard pressed to perform the latter.

Forecasts that point to events that are likely to happen may be more consistently reliable, but they have limited insight – and therefore limited value. What we really need to have on our radar are what Michael Oppenheimer, Professor of Geosciences and International Affairs at Princeton, terms big *strategy-invalidating* tipping points that can rewrite the rules of the game. These are the significant moments with the potential to radically rewire the world we live in and completely short-circuit existing strategies that were based on the status quo.

For example, after a fairly stable period of global economic growth, many businesses had expansionary strategies at the beginning of 2007. However, their plans were totally derailed by the global financial shock that started shortly thereafter. Very few people had ever heard of the sub-prime mortgages that triggered the crisis.

24

A few years later, in December 2010, life in Tunisia was upended when a street vendor set himself on fire after the authorities confiscated his goods. The resulting public anger and protests spread rapidly to Egypt, other parts of North Africa and the Middle East. Known as the Arab Spring, it became a general uprising by citizens against oppressive regimes in the region and has left its mark to this day.

When the first cases of Covid-19 showed up in Wuhan in December 2019, how many companies played out the scenario of lockdowns and empty high streets, or imagined that they could be forced to close their business temporarily (or even permanently) within the next four months? These kinds of events are few and far between, but given the enormity of their consequences, accepting them as risks has significant strategic value.

In a 1969 paper on foreign policy and intelligence, Thomas L. Hughes – assistant secretary of state for intelligence and research during the Kennedy and Johnson administrations – quotes the recollections of a retiree from the British Foreign Office, who served from 1903 to 1950: 'Year after year the worriers and the fretters would come to me with awful predictions of the outbreak of war. I denied it each time. I was wrong only twice.'

What this irony highlights – and what forecasters often miss – is that thinking the future is as much about *quality* as it is about *quantity*. Thinking the future is often judged by what we regularly get right, but consistently predicting likely occurrences is actually of limited value. The civil servant was right most of the time in dismissing the possibility of war (quantity), but he was wrong about *two world wars* (shamefully poor quality). Capturing the potential for game-changing events is what distinguishes the real strategic value of thinking the future from normal surmising about it. The conventional model of forecasting – based as it is on extrapolation and single-line projections with limited imagination – means that it is inherently ill-suited to capture these inflection points.

American entrepreneur and economist Roger Babson famously said on 5 September 1929: 'Sooner or later a crash is coming, and it may be terrific.' Wall Street crashed later that month, leading to the Great Depression of the 1930s. Notice one thing, though: the statement is qualified. He said 'may be terrific', not '*will* be terrific'. He captured the biggest economic event of the last century, but left room for error regarding the magnitude of the crash. Equally, he had ten commandments for investing. Among them were: don't be fooled by a name; don't buy without the proper facts; and safeguard purchases through diversification. Does that not sound like foxy thinking?

The point with both of these examples is that thinking the future effectively isn't necessarily gauged by the accuracy of the prediction, as we stated more briefly back in Chapter 1. Trying to be more accurate is important, but it's not the *end goal* of thinking the future. You can generally be very accurate and still miss a life-defining event. We should judge how effective we are at thinking the future by how much it informs our decision-making. Does it make us more prepared for life's challenges and opportunities, or not? Single-projection forecasts, however consistent they are in accuracy, set us up for an *expected future*. They can blind us rather than increase our awareness and are likely to leave us unprepared for moments that depart profoundly from the status quo. To be better prepared, we must continually question the assumptions underpinning our expectations, not resolutely cling to them.

Superficially, forecasts seem to be useful tools. After all, they do provide a blueprint for how the future may play out. But when you're trapped in a dark cave of uncertainty, you'll grab onto anything that sounds as if it has been properly researched. Instead, you should beware of forecasters who show unwonted confidence in their predictions. Have they *really* found the cat? Does the cat even exist?

Like foxes with all-round vision, we must be conscious of the fact that a single-line forecast represents *one* possibility for how the future may play out. In graphical terms, it is usually represented by a smooth curve with no inflection point to indicate that drama is on the way. Furthermore, each underlying assumption incorporated into the modelling behind that projection is vulnerable to being wrong too. Hardly comfortable odds if a significant amount of money or time is at stake.

Questioning our assumptions is a critical part of negotiating life's big hurdles. Curiosity may have killed the cat, but satisfaction brought it back. Similarly, for our hero Socrates, curiosity was something ultimately worth dying for too. But his legacy should bring us all the satisfaction of becoming better futurists. Curiosity has its perils, but it's worth it.

joke would be on the jury: his legacy has defined philosophic and scientific inquiry for millennia. His humble approach got right to the nub of good thinking, thereby exposing a very simple principle essential to thinking the future more effectively: question your assumptions at all times and without prejudice.

There are few areas of specialisation where this rationale is more important than in the dangerous world of intelligence.

An Unexamined Future Is Not Worth Contemplating

The intelligence community is full of professional thinkers about the future, where a bad day in the office could result in death or nuclear annihilation. Their job is to anticipate imminent and longer-term threats and opportunities. These could range from organised terror plots to lone-wolf attacks; from engaging in sophisticated cyberwarfare to shutting down bedroom-based hackers; all the way to monitoring the development of modern and often concealed arsenals in competing nation states. They then feed that information – analysed and packaged – to leading policy-shapers and decision-makers. From an organisational perspective, they're very good at structuring themselves to provide reports that are consistent, reliable and of actionable value. But to do this, the intelligence community needs to be fully aware of potential cognitive pitfalls, one of which commonly occurs in a process called layering.

In intelligence, layering is the practice of building assessments – such as reports on the likelihood of an attack – one on top of another. One of the problems is that each new assessment does not necessarily re-examine the uncertainties and ambiguities associated with the previous one. It is a bit like stacking Jenga bricks, but without first checking if the table you're stacking them on has a dodgy leg. Each brick may be sturdy and carefully stacked, but if the base upon which you're building the entire edifice is unstable, then the game could be over before it begins.

The build-up to the Iraq War that began in 2003 was one such example of a high-stakes Jenga game gone wrong. In 2002, the British Joint Intelligence Committee and the American National Intelligence Council each

31

prepared key assessments on the state of the Iraqi weapons programme. Specifically, they wanted to know if Iraqi president Saddam Hussein was building weapons of mass destruction and, if so, what level of threat these weapons posed to their respective nations in the future.

Both the British and American intelligence reports drew heavily on previous assessments. This is not problematic in itself. If resources are limited, starting afresh each time a new exercise is undertaken is unfeasible. Having said that, intelligence is often influenced by the circumstances pertaining at the time, meaning that some important qualifications may need to be borne in mind when a new assessment is produced at a later date. To use the Jenga analogy, you would want to know where the weak spots in your friend's old collapsible picnic table are before you start playing. Leaning too heavily on one corner may end the game.

A key attribute to qualifying every assessment is what the intelligence community calls validation. This means vetting each source and weighing up its credibility. As intelligence officers and analysts build a case, they double-check each constituent part to be as sure as they can of just how sturdy its structure is. Validation is incredibly important at the base level of intelligence collection – the so-called raw intelligence, such as first-hand accounts that function as foundational pillars. These critical pieces of information lend significant weight to the overall assessment. And this is where the British and American intelligence assessments were woefully fragile in the lead-up to the Iraq War.

But this only tells half the story. When speaking of global intelligence, we must identify the two broader groups of players involved. On the one side is what the intelligence community calls 'producers'. These individuals and organisations do what the label on the tin advertises: they produce the intelligence assessments through the collection, analysis and presentation of key information. To invoke a James Bond analogy, they're the Ms and Qs of the world. They produce a commodity for the other players involved: the consumers. These are the policy-shapers and decision-makers to whom the producers are ultimately accountable.

Just as in commercial market dynamics, there are push-and-pull forces emanating from each side of the policy process. The producers may push assessments that they think consumers should know about, but they prion the ones that pertain to the topic around which you are constructing possible futures. Moreover, they should be prioritised in terms of relevance, so that you do not end up with too formidable a list, full of items that are more distracting than helpful in your planning. No matter what field of interest you're investigating, though, we insist that there are always ethical rules to honour, and you must inspect your ethical compass for guidance around which rules are relevant to the exercise in hand.

This can be difficult, as the ethical domain sometimes stretches well beyond the official laws and regulations written in black and white. It is about what you *ought* to do in addition to what you are legally obliged to do. As you will read later, the conduct of some companies has fallen foul of these rules for too long, but the past will catch up with them someday. Occasionally, when the public is sufficiently enraged, CEOs pay the price by having to resign for disregarding the ethical compass.

On to step two: select the *key uncertainties*. These are forces that can have a variety of possible outcomes and consequences for the future you are considering, sometimes with the capacity to drive it in opposite directions. The winner of the 2020 US presidential election was a key uncertainty for US and international politics until the results were announced in November. There were two possible outcomes, and the consequences would have been vastly different if Donald Trump had been re-elected.

As you can tell from the term, key uncertainties are unpredictable, to varying degrees. Accordingly, the narratives flowing out of them can be spread far and wide. In the metaphor of musical chairs, you would not be able to say, before switching on the torch again, who is going to be sitting in which chair and who is going to be left standing when the music stops. That is because the behaviour of the people in the room, who are themselves groping around in semi-darkness, is a key uncertainty beyond your control.

Let's examine an example closer to home. In new personal relationships, the behaviour of the other person can be a key uncertainty until you get to know them better. If that person proves to be inherently impulsive, you might find yourself playing scenarios of what could happen every time you meet. In sport and business, competitor strategy is an obvious key uncertainty.

Climate change as an overarching force is a rule of the game, but our collective response to it is a key uncertainty. Hence, the *rate* of climate change is also a key uncertainty because it depends on our collective response. At the time of writing, the length and severity of the coronavirus pandemic is still a key uncertainty, despite the vaccination programmes taking place around the world. Further waves of infection continue to challenge societies, and new variants of the virus pose additional risks. It is quite conceivable that humanity will soon face a new virus altogether.

Barring a major surprise, China is due to overtake America as the largest economy in the world in the not-too-distant future. The future relationship between the two countries is therefore a key uncertainty. One is an autocracy and the other a democracy. How might the rest of the world react to having a new nation with a completely different culture as its head? How will America take it? How will issues like fair trade, intellectual property rights, the treatment of the Uighurs in China, the future status of Taiwan and Hong Kong, and China's increasing military presence in the South China Sea, play out? Will an alliance be formed between the world's leading democracies to persuade China to change its behaviour? The answers to all these questions are up in the air.

The third step in Wack's model for re-perception is to paint different *scenarios* of what can happen, using the rules and uncertainties as the basic structure. Given the origin of the term 'scenario planning' and the fact that they must connect with their audience, we feel that it is appropriate to think of scenarios as movie scripts of the future. Their narratives must be logical, but they also need *oomph*.

Giving the scenario a great title is one way to make decision-makers lean forward in their seats. Good storytelling will elicit 'oohs' and 'ahs' as they see where the twists and turns of key uncertainties could lead. The audience then leaves the scenario theatre with the feeling of having been transported through a realm of possibilities, and the outside world no longer looks quite the same. Scenarios, when done right, will make you re-perceive reality. The pattern of forces propelling us into the future suddenly becomes clear, and illusions are dispelled.

This effect can be felt even if, in a mode of self-reflection, you are the star of the stories you produce yourself, plotting out the paths your own future can take. You are the most important audience member as well, and it's important that you be gripped by what you see so that you make the decisions you would want your main character to make.

This movie metaphor also applies to a board of directors scripting their own company's possible futures. They just need a good facilitator who, like an inspiring film director, will liberate their imaginations and make them feel like the protagonists of the stories they've constructed.

A really powerful, vivid scenario can sometimes help to create the future it sketches. There is nothing wrong with that, providing it is the best-case and not the worst-case scenario we're talking about. At the same time, a dystopian movie script graphically describing a worst-case scenario can alert the participants to the possibility of stumbling into disaster if they do not take preventative action now. This is essentially what Herman Kahn did: turn an inconvenient truth into something that had to be acknowledged and resolved. Today's scenario planners could plot out the frightening consequences of ongoing misogyny, racism, deepening inequality and the blatant exploitation of cheap labour in a style that would get the approval of prize-winning novelists.

In developing scenarios with clients, we have learnt that coming up with too many scenarios can cause analysis paralysis. Our recommendation is that you keep things clear and simple by following one of two approaches. The first is to pick the two key uncertainties that are most crucial to the future you are considering. Let's say you want to change careers, and the rule of the game is that you need a degree to do so. There are lots of factors involved, but you decide that the two most important ones are completing your studies in the time specified and getting financial support from your partner while you study.

You will need to narrow the outcome of these uncertainties to two possibilities each – an either/or. In our example, either you get the degree or you don't, and your partner either covers all the finances or they don't. Then, you use the two uncertainties and their outcomes to construct a matrix with four quadrants. Plot one uncertainty along the vertical axis, and the other along the horizontal axis. It would look like this:

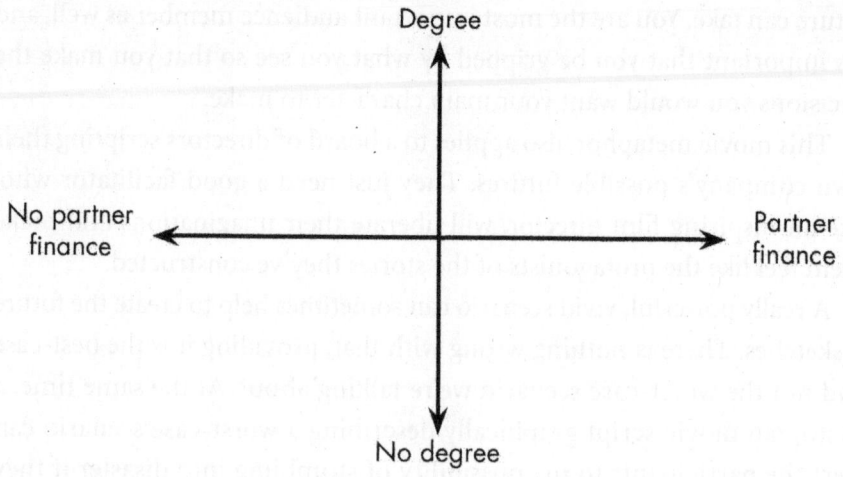

This gives you a visual representation of four possible scenarios. There will most likely be a best-case scenario, where the outcomes of both uncertainties are positive, and a worst-case scenario, where both uncertainties have negative outcomes. The other two scenarios will constitute a middle-ground or compromise, where a positive outcome in one uncertainty meets a negative outcome in another.

The best-case scenario in our example is to get the degree and the financial support and enter a bright future in a new career. In one middle-ground scenario, your partner loses their job or ends the relationship, and although you get your degree, you have loans to repay because you lost your financial support. In a similarly bittersweet scenario, your studies prove too challenging, and you fail or drop out, but because your partner can continue paying the bills, you can plan for an alternative career. Finally, in the worst-case scenario, you fail to get your degree and you can no longer depend on your partner's income, so you need a new job as soon as possible or try to get your old job back.

In some scenario exercises, you will find that the good outcome of one key uncertainty will conflict with the bad outcome of the other, because they cannot coexist in the real world. For example, the two uncertainties between a pair of nations might be whether they will trade more with one another in future, or less, and whether they will go to war with one another or stay at peace. Obviously, they wouldn't go to war *and* increase trade with other. Kahn considered this policy rather questionable, and to illustrate his point he created the concept of a 'Doomsday Machine' that would destroy all life on earth if anyone launched a nuclear attack on America. If this sounds familiar, it's because it inspired *Dr Strangelove*, Stanley Kubrick's satirical take on the Cold War and fears of a nuclear conflict. The lead character is based partially on Kahn himself, and some of the dialogue comes from *On Thermonuclear War*.

Both controversial and alarming, the book nevertheless got the rapt attention of American and Soviet military planners and could not have been published at a better time. The Cuban Missile Crisis, involving a confrontation between the US and the Soviet Union over Soviet missile deployment in Cuba, happened two years later, in October 1962. With mis-understandings on both sides, it was, and remains, the moment the two military superpowers came closest to a nuclear conflict. Thanks partially to Khan's detailed scenarios of world war, megadeath and post-apocalyptic life, disaster was avoided.

Wack felt that scenario planning could open people's minds in the business sector, just as Kahn had done in the fields of military strategy and national security policy. He took issue with the simplistic futures thinking that management usually relied upon and said that forecasts 'often work because the world does not always change. But sooner or later forecasts will fail when they are needed most: in anticipating major shifts in the business environment that make whole strategies obsolete.'

Along with his colleague Ted Newland, known for his incisive opinions on social and political issues, Wack established a scenario-planning division at Royal Dutch Shell's head office in London in the 1970s. They pioneered the process in an industrial setting.

Their team successfully captured the oil-price shocks of 1973 and 1979. However, the first set of scenarios, which included the 1973 oil-crisis scenario, did not lead to any shift in the company's strategy or tactics. Wack realised that scenarios were not worth the paper they were written on if the decision-makers took no real notice of them. He would often quote Paul Valéry, a twentieth-century French philosopher, on the import-ance of perception: 'A fact poorly observed is more treacherous than faulty reasoning.'

Thus, Wack embarked on a quest to get people to re-perceive the world around them so that they would see it in its true light and accept that sometimes it behaved like a capricious animal, capable of unpredictable outbursts of behaviour. To achieve his goal, he first had to find a way of communicating his ideas so that they sunk in. He initiated a study of Shell's prevailing culture and started by interviewing the Shell managers one by one to explore what he called their 'microcosm', namely their mental model of the 'macrocosm' – the real world around them. Unless he understood that in advance, his team's scenario presentations would fall on deaf ears and be irrelevant for strategy.

A 1972 survey had shown that thirty-eight out of the forty most senior managers at Shell believed that the price of oil would rise from its current level of \$1.80 per barrel to \$2 per barrel in 1980. From his interviews, Wack learnt that even after the 1973 oil crisis, during which the price of oil rose almost four times, from \$3 per barrel to nearly \$12 per barrel in March 1974, the majority opinion of Shell executives was that the market would settle down again.

Armed with a better feel for management's collective microcosm and the language they used in describing it, Wack's subsequent scenario exercises proved much more influential. They struck a chord in the executives' internal world and made them aware of how the external world – namely the global oil market – could evolve in unexpected ways. The rules of the game had changed, and by accepting that, the executives were better equipped to tackle the commercial challenges posed by the market.

What was once improbable to management became thinkable, and through various innovative measures, Shell took full advantage of the second oil-price shock, in 1979, when the price of oil more than doubled to nearly \$40 a barrel in early 1980. The reward for the company was huge.

When it comes to thinking the future, of course, it is not just about selling your ideas to someone else – it is about selling them to yourself. You have to examine your own mental images and models to see how much they accord with reality. And remember this: poor observations can catch you out just as much as poor reasoning. Let us therefore introduce you to Wack's model, so that you can become the scenario planner and the audience at the same time.

A Simple Model for Re-perceiving the Future

Wack devised a simple three-step formula for scenario planning. This approach applies as much to an individual looking ahead at career choices and where to live as it does to an executive team in a business, or other type of organisation, trying to envisage the best strategy to cope with changes in the industry or environment around them. It also applies to a government imagining how the world economy may change in order to optimise its own domestic economic policies.

As we said in Chapter 1, Wack did not like the idea of forecasting, because it was like shining a torch into a dim room where people were playing musical chairs. You could turn the torch on, switch it off and not have a clue where people would be sitting the next time you turned it on again. That brief glimpse might help if nobody moved but would be useless if they did. Nevertheless, there's one thing you could be sure of if you were standing by the door and it was the only escape route: as long as nobody passed you on their way in or out, the number of people in the room would stay the same.

Figuring out the factors you can be sure of is the first step in Wack's method. He called these factors 'predetermined elements', and we call them the *rules of the game*, because they establish a firm foundation for thinking the future. These elements or rules are safe assumptions that you can make about the future that will hold true under any circumstances – not quite as absolute as the laws of mathematics, but relatively fixed patterns you feel confident about. They are the things that will stay the same while everything else might be changing.

Of course, you would need to subject those assumptions to searching questions, as Socrates recommended, before accepting them as the basis for further inquiry into the future. Moreover, as the Stoics would say, the rules of the game lie in the circle beyond your control; if you had the power to change them on a whim, they wouldn't be rules. They're similar to the ones you'd find in any sport: you can have only eleven players on each side in a game of cricket or soccer, and you have to keep the ball between certain lines on a tennis court. In the musical-chairs metaphor, there is one assertion you can make for all the scenarios you could dream up: the numbers will remain the same as long as no one enters or leaves the room.

In normal life, the rules change more than they do in sport, so what you are looking for are rules that will *almost certainly* apply in the future, regardless of what applied in the past. In professional life, for example, highly skilled careers require specific qualifications. This is a rule that won't change, although the list of required qualifications might. If you're in the market to buy property, you'll know that house prices depend on the status of the area you wish to live in. That factor isn't likely to change either, but it's important to check if the status of the area is undergoing a revision.

In business, existing or forthcoming legislation can be considered part of the rules for the future of the industry concerned. For governments, the rules would include the laws of international trade or finance, but there may be amendments in the pipeline that will constitute rules in the future. The term 'rules-based international order' is now used frequently by national leaders to indicate their desired objective. In all these cases, from the smallest to the biggest game, the rules are factors with very specific consequences.

Trends may be considered rules if they are strong enough, although they are not as fixed, and their effects are more debatable. The advice for exercising and eating to stay in good health seems to change every year, although those in the fitness and wellness industries can still rely on broad principles while capitalising on fads. New technologies shape the way business is practised, from the way ATMs changed the role of bank branches in the 1970s to the way online marketing is currently changing shopping.

In politics and economics, the ageing populations of rich countries is a trend that predictably slows down economic growth rates, while social media use must now be considered an important factor in driving populist and nationalist movements.

Playing by the rules is the only way to participate in the game of scenario planning, and you may also need the latest rules to *win* the game, whatever that might mean to you as an individual or for a company or nation. Ignore the rules, and you are effectively ignoring the ways in which reality works. The scenarios you plan will be meaningless and you will be penalised like players in sport.

When identifying the rules of the game, you should, of course, focus marily try to service the requests of the consumers – the pull. After all, intelligence agencies are in the business of providing information of action-able value to decision-makers.

This push-and-pull relationship does not only exist in the worlds of intelligence, politics and economics. It's also the model of information-gathering in our everyday lives. We often search for information to inform specific decisions. In those instances, we're the pull. At other times, important information is pushed to us, perhaps by friends, families or colleagues. Or we're the ones pushing information to others. Being aware of the dynamics involved when we exchange information reminds us that the process is rarely neutral. Our demand for information might mean we're susceptible to anything that affirms our beliefs, and wary of information that doesn't. Those who feed us information might have the best intentions, but they're not necessarily neutral in their own motivations either. And, of course, we're all familiar with the practice of telling people what they want to hear.

In the lead-up to the 2003 invasion of Iraq, there was a strong pull effect from the politicians. US president George W. Bush and British prime minister Tony Blair were committed to war, and hence were looking for arguments to support their case, most notably the existence of weapons of mass destruction in Iraq. They were driven by one central idea, and in their public speeches they incorporated evidence to support that idea without fully entertaining different perspectives on how the future could play out. In a word, they were being hedgehogs. It was a dangerous and irresponsible gamble.

If weapons of mass destruction *had* been found in Iraq, thus proving Bush and Blair correct, then history would perhaps reflect more favourably on their decision to go to war. However, this misses the point: the process behind their decision-making was flawed, and it would have been luck, rather than skill, that rewarded them. The characteristic that distinguishes good futures thinking from poor futures thinking is a consistent review process. And entertaining multiple perspectives to question one's assump-tions is critical to making that process effective over time. New evidence should be allowed to influence your judgement of reality to bring it into line with the moving reality of the situation as much as possible. And that judgement may change with the next review.

Although Bush, Blair and the politicians around them predictably fell into the trap of confirmation bias, the exact opposite of the process we have just described, the intelligence producers didn't escape the pull of the politicians; they fell into the trap too. One of the striking revelations of the first major inquiry into the intelligence failure – Lord Butler's 'Review of Intelligence of Weapons of Mass Destruction', completed in 2004 – was the lack of reliable human-agent reporting. There were no first-hand accounts from British secret service agents of any nuclear, biological, chemical or ballistic missile programmes in Iraq.

Invoking your inner Socrates, you have to ask yourself how supposedly respected intelligence agencies could have made such an obvious mistake. The answer is that they started with a misguided assumption: that militaristic dictators would naturally wish to acquire weapons of mass destruction, and there was no reason why Saddam Hussein would have abandoned any capability he did have.

At the time it didn't seem ludicrous to base future scenarios on this assumption. Then again, the most dangerous assumptions are the ones that sound like common sense. They're the assertions we're more likely to take for granted *because* they seem reasonable to us – and that's where the trouble lies. The comfort we find in an assertion's apparent reasonableness dissuades us from challenging it.

The Chilcot report, which was published in 2016 and comprehensively covered Britain's role in the Iraq War, was equally damning. It highlighted how the layering of each new intelligence assessment by the various agencies made matters worse. The misguided assumptions, based on scant evidence, were not filed away in some cabinet to be forgotten. Rather, they became the foundations underpinning a tower of Jenga bricks. Furthermore, the lack of validation for each new layer of bricks meant that the basic intelligence flaws travelled up through the assessment structure, to be yanked out at the top by politicians yearning for justification.

We have dealt at great length with the intelligence failure in the lead-up to the Iraq War because it provides a cogent example of how misguided assumptions can shape the nature of our beliefs and lead to, or exacerbate, poor decision-making. Thinking the future demands continually asking the right questions to expose frailties hiding in the shadows of any assertion.

But how do you know which are the right and wrong questions to ask? Socrates's fundamental principle of authentic desire for understanding is key, and a good place to start is to reflect on what you hope to get out of a forthcoming decision. Highlighting your end goal can help draw attention to the ways in which you might be focusing on information that fits your agenda.

At the same time, you need to pinch yourself to take more notice of the details you are trying to avoid, because they will undermine your goal. That, in turn, can provide you with a reality check so that you probe your assumptions properly. There will be a greater degree of neutrality in the questions you raise with yourself and encourage others to ask you.

To be sure, if a British equivalent of Socrates were ever to become M, they would launch a major shake-up of MI6 to ensure that the chances of being so confidently wrong again were reduced to a minimum. We should all learn from our mistakes, and probably the most important lesson from the Iraq episode is that pleasing your customer – which may work in business – is a major handicap in matters of national or global intelligence.

There has to be a clear separation of powers between the intelligence community and the government it serves, so that information cannot be massaged to the satisfaction of those higher up the hierarchical ladder. Obviously, they should respect and communicate with one another, but not at the expense of independence of thought among intelligence producers.

Intelligence professionals are there to provide a mental model of the world that matches the fundamentals of the real one as accurately as possible. The politicians are there to recalibrate their internal compasses if required to do so by the facts as presented. That way they are less likely to get their fingers burned. The retort may be that advisers advise and ministers decide. It does not alter the fact that decisions based on impartial advice, delivered in a cool-headed manner, prove correct more often than those that aren't.

At the same time, from an internal perspective, every tier of the intelligence structure needs to have a duty of curiosity about a case being handed to it by a lower tier. In particular, the quality of the evidence has to be examined with an open mind. This means engaging in a Socratic dialogue where the conversation resembles that of one in a court of law:

the prosecution offers one interpretation or scenario of the case in hand, the defence argues for an alternative, and the validation of sources has the same level of energy as the cross-examination of witnesses.

The tag-team of questioning and assertion is allowed to operate with sufficient intensity for biases to be demolished and the essence of the matter to be explored. Bitterness and tension should not be allowed to invade the debate. Think of it as a no-holds-barred peer review that scientists and medical experts undergo all the time when publishing new material.

We are not saying that this approach guarantees a much higher level of certainty in the knowledge regarding a particular threat. The final judgement can still be qualified by the method of assigning a probability as to how likely information is to be true or false. Indeed, this process is no different to the principle in civil litigation where the burden of proof is based on the balance of probabilities. In criminal trials, a higher standard is required, as the evidence must prove beyond reasonable doubt that the accused committed the crime for the guilty verdict to be given. Seldom do future-threat assessments in the intelligence world get anywhere near to that requirement.

Doubt is inherent in prediction. Hence, the Socratic approach, which embraces doubt, will improve the odds that the finished product handed to the ultimate consumer, in this case the UK government, is of higher quality than the information used to justify the invasion of Iraq. Why? Because MI6 will be starting to think the future like a fox.

Finally, a Socratic M would probably change the recruitment policies of MI6 to attract a wider range of talent in light of the evolving intelligence game. Spying would expand from secretly obtaining information on the enemy to discerning, by careful observation, all the other possible threats to the security and safety of citizens – including pandemics, climate change and disinformation. Socratic inquisitiveness is a necessary condition for capturing the complexity and dynamic nature of the big picture, and then drawing out the implications for the consumer. The latter will then have the responsibility of taking action to grab the opportunities and counter the threats.

Ignore the need for structurally sound knowledge and you risk building what eighteenth-century British philosopher Jeremy Bentham termed swan? Do you know something about the biology of a swan that prevents it from being any other colour? Do you trust that the people who told you swans are white know what they're talking about?

We know now what a mistake it was to assume the universal whiteness of swans, but for hundreds of years Europeans would have considered it trivial and ignorant to question that assumption. They believed all swans were white, having heard of no other colour until the seventeenth century, when Dutch explorer Willem de Vlamingh sailed to Australia and discovered black swans. The lesson of the swan analogy is that our assertions are only ever as good as our attempts to question them. Questioning prepares the sails and gets us out and exploring.

It helps to think of questioning and assertion as a tag team. We wouldn't get far in the world if we questioned absolutely everything and never put a stake in the ground. Questions need something to work with, so we make assertions and use questioning to test the strength of those assertions (or at least, we *should*). As in any tag team, relying too much on one raises the risk of undermining the other – and that makes for an unhealthy team dynamic.

If you leave questioning out of the ring, then assertion will try to take on the world without its teammate. Life may appear simpler than it is, and without any checks and balances, assertion will run riot. But its sustainability will be limited. Eventually, when assertion tries to do some heavy lifting, it will discover the limit of its strength. Grappling with questioning gives assertion its grit. So, rather than discouraging it, make questioning part of the team, especially when preparing for those big, strategic changes in your life. Questions are likely to stimulate a robust, multifaceted view of what the future may hold.

Equally, questioning can't get to grips with life's greatest mysteries on its own. If it gets on a roll without assertion, then before long you will get caught in a tailspin and become riddled with doubt. Like a child, your plans or predictions will climb into bed, turn off the lights and go to sleep. Assertion must eventually have its day, unless you want to go down as a permanent ditherer or, worse still, a professional fence-sitter.

All in all, the Socratic method is a well-balanced tag-team effort between questioning and assertion. The strength and robustness of each assertion is tested and qualified by a bout of questioning. When assertion comes through the other side, it is stronger for it. Socrates was the ultimate trainer. His gift to philosophy was illustrating the role and importance of a rugged training regime for each and every assertion. This is what distinguishes robust science from pseudoscience, good historians from misguided ones, and, ultimately, what distinguishes good futures thinking from pure speculation.

You may be thinking: What differentiates good probing questions from annoying, time-wasting ones? There's an art to it – which Socrates mastered over time. But he kept things very, very simple. What set his approach apart from others was an *authentic* desire for understanding. Questions just designed to prove someone wrong should be reserved for debating competitions. They have little value beyond temporarily affirming one's self-perceived superiority and upsetting the opposing team. Being guided by a genuine desire to bolster the robustness of your argument will prompt the right questions. To help facilitate the process, be foxy and try to entertain multiple perspectives – this will expose knowledge you might otherwise have missed.

Socrates's deep questioning found him on the wrong side of the authorities in Athens. At his trial, facing charges associated with challenging the status quo, he continued, undaunted, to play the devil's advocate. He stressed the importance of questioning assumptions right up to the moment he was sentenced to death. For all of ancient Athens's progressive qualities in art, music, politics and philosophy, the jury that sealed Socrates's verdict just couldn't face being unsettled to the extent that he saw necessary. Few people enjoy confronting the boundaries of their knowledge, beyond which they have to confess ignorance or doubt. Ironically, that same confrontation has fuelled innovation since the beginning of humankind – it's the most important determinant underpinning progress. We must find comfort in that and remind ourselves of doubt's role each time we feel uneasy about challenges to our system of beliefs.

Socrates could have got off the hook if he had given in and made a commitment to change his ways. But for him, an unexamined life just wasn't worth living. To take away his wonder would have been to take away his essence. He lived and died for the right to question everything. But the

Consulting the Oracle

If you could ask an oracle just one question about the future, what would it be? If you were putting it to the oracle at Delphi in ancient Greece, you would have needed to slaughter an animal just to earn the privilege of her ear. Plus, you would have probably had to wait for the seventh day of the month, when the Pythia – the high priestess who served as the oracle by consulting the god Apollo – was in. Apparently, she also didn't operate during winter months, when Apollo was away. Foretelling the future has always been a tough job. Pilgrims were likely to walk away scratching their heads thanks to cleverly worded prophecies. The latter were effectively unfalsifiable because they were open to multiple interpretations. Nevertheless, the ancient Greeks would've cut Apollo some slack since he was spread pretty thinly across all his commitments. He was the god of sun and light, music and poetry, healing and plagues, archery, agriculture, knowledge and, of course, prophecy – a LinkedIn profile for the ages that would do him proud today.

Delphi was perched high up on the slopes of Mount Parnassus, about 180 kilometres north-west of Athens. While you waited for your prophecy, you could take in the amazing view, or watch a play at the local theatre framed by an empyrean backdrop. Alternatively, you could have visited the Omphalos of Delphi – a conical stone that supposedly marked the earth's navel. As legend had it, Zeus threw two eagles into the sky, one to the east and the other to the west and instructed them to fly towards each other. Directly below where they crossed, Zeus planted a stone in the earth. That spot would become the Omphalos of Delphi, marking the centre of the world.

If you weren't quite up to slaughtering an animal, or were in a bit of a rush, the oracle could perform the ancient equivalent of a drive-through service. You could pop in for a quick take, as long as you were going to ask a 'yes or no' type of question. Prophecy is a lot easier when the scope is narrowed to just two possible options.

All this preamble brings us to one of Plato's seminal works, the *Apology of Socrates*. From it, we hear that Chaerephon, a loyal friend of Socrates, made the journey up the steep hill to see the Oracle of Delphi. Luckily for him – and the oracle – he had one simple question on his mind: Is there anyone wiser than Socrates?

The Pythian priestess gave Chaerephon a definite no – there was no one wiser than Socrates. Chaerephon was not surprised; anyone who knew Socrates would have wagered a few drachmas that he was among the top five intellects in town. But there was someone shocked to hear the news: Socrates. He had always considered himself lacking in knowledge, so how on earth could he be the wisest man around?

To test this proposition, he wandered around the forum in ancient Athens, asking supposedly knowledgeable people searching questions about themselves and human existence. Those he questioned seemed to offer convincing answers at first, but upon further enquiry, that conviction unravelled. Socrates realised that they were laying claim to knowledge they didn't have. He reflected further and concluded that the oracle might have been seriously perspicacious in her reply. Surely, he thought, it's better to be aware of your lack of knowledge than to think you know something when you actually don't. Perhaps the oracle meant that no one was wiser than him because he, more than anyone else, understood the limits of his own knowledge.

It is perhaps that clarity of insight that Raphael tried to capture in the painting we mentioned in Chapter 1 – the *School of Athens*. Socrates is in it too, dressed in green, standing just to the left of Plato and Aristotle. He's portrayed in action, mid-debate, pointing to his fingers as if adding up the premises of an argument. The suggestion is that by the time he gets to his pinkie, his debating counterparts are going to see the error of their ways, the flaws in their assumptions.

But for all its subsequent fame, the method of enquiry Socrates employed was quite simple: question the assumptions underlying each belief until any hidden contradictions or absurdities come to the surface. Pass this test, and you might be onto something. This approach, later termed the Socratic method, is the distinguishing mark of a true philosopher – literally a lover of wisdom. That's because it places questioning at the heart of its methodological approach. It is rooted in wonder and curiosity. There's a moral here for all involved in the future-scanning profession.

Questioning is the opposite of assertion – the forecaster's tool of trade. Assertion presupposes a belief of some kind. You might assert, for example, that all swans are white. Questioning encourages doubt: Have you seen every 'nonsense upon stilts', or what futurists call pure speculation. Speculation can be easy, and often serves those with questionable intentions. After all, no one can hold you to account right now, when the future is yet to happen. But it's just as easy for you to fall foul of your own beliefs if you've built them on a fragile base without knowing it. Our misguided assumptions often go unchallenged because of their apparent reasonableness. Therefore, we constantly need to be on a Socratic footing to root out frail foundations when thinking the future and evaluating our personal projects.

Remember this the next time you are contemplating the future for yourself, especially if you are both the producer and consumer of information. You ought to have a meaningful internal dialogue before taking action.

The lessons of this chapter are fundamental to our philosophy, so before we proceed to some questions, we'll summarise the key points:

- The complexity and uncertainty of the future can have you grabbing on to comfortable expectations, false certainties and deep longings rather than facing your doubts.
- Good futures thinking comes from good thinking practices.
- Don't take your knowledge for granted, even when it seems reasonable. Learn to question the assumptions underlying your assertions and decisions.
- Assess the quality and validity of your information and its sources.
- Last but not least, be wary of the trap that is confirmation bias.

Now, let's stir you into thinking like Socrates:

1. Do you follow any explicit thought process when making big decisions? For example, do you regularly consult friends and family and consider their advice, even if it differs from your own? Do you weigh up the pros and cons? If you want to do something, do you develop a counterargument as to why you *shouldn't* do it?
2. The next time you read an opinion piece, try to find a related piece from a very different news source – one typically associated with different political views. Weigh up the two perspectives and ask yourself: How much of my belief system is shaped by the arguments contained therein and how much by my existing preferences? If I were to find a middle ground between these views, what would it be?

3. Now that you've been introduced to the Socratic method, what confident assertions, which you regularly make in conversations about the future with the people around you, will you test more robustly with outside sources?

4. When talking about the future, do you ever tell people what they want to hear and entertain their misguided assumptions, perhaps to protect yourself or nurture relationships? Given that it can be more comforting to choose certainty over doubt and have your beliefs confirmed rather than undermined, are you willing to be more honest, curious and questioning? What factors would make you more or less likely to challenge your assumptions and those of others?

5. Have you ever had a conversation that made you revise some basic belief in your life? What were – or could be – the long-term consequences of that shift in perspective?

Chapter 3

What Can You Control?

Never let the future disturb you. You will meet it, if you have to, with the same weapons of reason which today arm you against the present.
Marcus Aurelius

We began this book with a fundamental distinction between two different ways of making sense of the world. On the one hand, foxes entertain multiple perspectives and try to understand things for what they are, without trying to include them in, or exclude them from, any one unitary inner vision. On the other hand, hedgehogs are more singular in their thinking, relating everything to one central idea. Given the complexity and uncertainty surrounding the future, we made a case for thinking like a fox.

Socrates then showed us the importance of testing the foundations of our thinking by questioning our assertions and assumptions. By doing so, we can see whether we've structured our vision of the future on solid observations and arguments or based it on thin air and hope. Being questioned on that vision may reveal the need to align it more closely with reality or stimulate us to revise our opinion of the principal forces that are changing the present into the future.

The previous chapter also stressed the importance of asking the right questions concerning the validity of expert predictions and how they were formulated. Intelligence in both the secret world of spies and the ordinary world we know has one thing in common: it is generally made up of *incomplete* information. Doubt plays an essential role in the discovery process – it's required to ask the searching questions and to dial back excessive confidence in a given outcome. If fact-checking has become an obsession in the media to see if someone is telling the truth about the past, then statements about the future demand even greater scrutiny.

However, let's not forget that we are actors as well as observers, and the future isn't completely outside of our control. Some things we can influence, others we can't. This distinction is critical to improving our understanding of the risks we face and then making smart strategic decisions to manage them. Here we can learn a lot from the Stoics, for whom the distinction between what we can and cannot control was fundamental. The opening quote of this chapter comes from Marcus Aurelius, who ruled Rome from 161 to 180 AD. He was the last emperor of Pax Romana, an age of relative peace and stability for the Roman Empire. More importantly, he was a Stoic philosopher whose matter-of-factness and fortitude are qualities that can steady us on the seas ahead.

The Quiet in the Storm

Imagine this: you're out at sea, in the middle of nowhere, clutching the mast of a ship at the centre of a terrific storm. Towering waves rise up and crash over you. Relentless, piercing rain pelts down from all angles. Booms of thunder bounce around your skull as if it were a pinball machine. Ominous charcoal clouds stretch to the end of the horizon, and you see no way for the captain to steer you out of trouble. There's every chance you might die.

How would you feel? What thoughts would be racing through your mind? Which of your emotions would be rising to the surface? Chances are you would be in a state of panic. How we feel is often tied to our circumstances, so in scary situations we feel frightened. In frustrating pickles we feel angry, and at times of loss we feel sad. Our emotions are dependent variables, to borrow a statistical term, sometimes switching from one extreme to another in a matter of seconds.

The story of Stoicism starts on a ship in a storm, when Zeno of Citium – a wealthy merchant in ancient Greece – was on a voyage between Phoenicia and Peiraeus. Onboard was his precious cargo: a royal purple dye that had to be painstakingly extracted from thousands of decaying murex sea snails. The storm took its toll. Zeno was washed ashore, but unfortunately his ship was not, and he lost everything. Nevertheless, his misfortune set him off on a new journey.

Zeno ended up in Athens, penniless and dressed in rags. One day he stumbled into a bookshop and, at random, picked up a copy of *Memorabilia* by Xenophon, a close friend and distinguished student of Socrates. The book's portrayal of Socrates left Zeno so hungry for more that he asked the bookseller where philosophers such as Socrates could be found. It just so happened that Crates of Thebes, a famous Cynic philosopher, was walking past, so the bookseller pointed to him.

Meeting Crates set Zeno off on a journey of philosophical discovery. Through introspection and observing the world around him, he developed his thinking, and eventually the student became the master. Zeno discussed his ideas while standing on a prominent porch near the Agora in Athens, and it was here that he fashioned his newfound perspective into a full-blown philosophical theory. The porch was the Stoa Poikile and the philosophy was about the relationship between our external circumstances and our reaction to them.

The Stoics, as Zeno and his students would later be called, in reference to their porch of origin, made their name by reimagining that relationship. Like most ancient Greek philosophers, they wanted to understand how we can lead happy and fulfilling lives. Quite controversially, they saw our emotional dependence on circumstances and the material world as genuine impediments to this pursuit. They asked: If how we feel is continually shaped by the external situation we find ourselves in, and many of those situations are tough, what control do we actually have over our happiness?

If such a question elicits fear and deep-seated worry, the attitude we adopt is the antidote. The Stoic on board a storm-tossed ship would be resolute in the face of adversity. As the clouds darkened and the wind howled, he would find quiet in the storm. The towering waves crashing against the ship? Nothing he can do about it. The thunder and the rain? Beyond his control. What is he, relative to the might of nature? He would clutch the mast to be as steady as he could. He would then acknowledge that panic would not do him or anyone else any good. It wouldn't change the weather or buttress the ship. However, calming his mind and focusing on what he *could* control would strengthen his ability to deal with what comes next.

The key ingredient to this Stoic resolve is a clear distinction between what is within and outside one's scope of control. If Zeno had been a management consultant, he would have grabbed a nearby stick and drawn in the sand an ancient form of that staple of modern-day PowerPoint presentations: the Venn diagram. Zeno's Venn diagram might have looked like this:

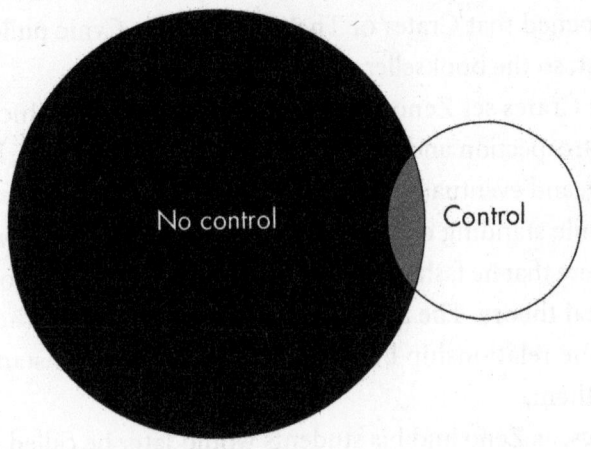

The circle representing that over which we have no control is significantly larger than the other. It includes not only things such as the weather, the economy, politics, and what other people think, say and do, but most of the interactions we have with the environment around us. The balance of power is not on our side. It doesn't matter how hard we clench our fists and hope or pray: if it's going to rain, it's going to rain. If the economy is heading south, one person can't turn it around with sheer ambition and drive.

Whether we like it or not, almost every aspect of the external world is beyond our influence. This may seem obvious, but it was the Stoics' ability to translate this awareness into thought and action that separated them from the rest of humanity. Instead of seeing ourselves as being at the mercy of forces beyond our control, a simple rational flip can immunise our internal constitution from feelings of panic, fear and hopelessness.

This rational flip and its immunising qualities are achieved by understanding the scope of the second circle: the things we *do* control. It's small – the Stoics believed it didn't consist of much. Indeed, the circle mainly contains just one thing: our judgement. But this is the one thing that really matters, because it alone has the capacity to constrain our emotions. *We* can decide what we *think* of the situations we find ourselves in. If we're stuck in traffic due to an accident ahead, and start running late for an important meeting, it's our *choice* to get angry and slap the steering wheel at the apparent cosmic design of the inconvenience. If we resent a colleague's verbal innuendo, accompanied by a snicker, it's our *choice* whether to respond or not.

Equally, it's our choice to refrain from resentment or anger and compulsive action in all situations. The agency lies with us. Our judgement is where the buck stops. Each emotional response may feel natural at the time, but the Stoics believed the causal chain from *incident* to *emotion* to *action* was breakable if we swung the axe just right and exercised our capacity to control ourselves.

This brings us to the overlap of the two circles – that little sliver over which we do not have complete control, but where we have *influence*. The overlap represents where our judgements inform our actions, which in turn can shape, to a limited extent, what's external to us. The Stoic in the storm couldn't do anything about the extreme weather – located as it was in the circle of no control – so he focused his mind and judgement on what he could do to be resilient in the situation. He concentrated on his circle of control.

In terms of influence, he could have lowered or raised the sail depending on the conditions dictated by the storm. But he would have needed to recognise the limits of his power against nature. Lowering the sail would mean spending longer in the storm and the boat could capsize. Raising the sail in an attempt to escape the storm would risk the sail being destroyed by the intense wind. This would have put him in another predicament: What would he do if the storm passed and he had no sail to continue his journey? Being motionless in the water could kill him too. Although there are no easy choices, thinking the future in this way – balancing what is in and outside his control and playing through scenarios – the Stoic sailor can steer his attention away from paralysing fear towards helpful decisions and action.

Amongst Stoics, the name Epictetus holds special prominence. He was a former slave who went on to become one of the foremost teachers of Stoicism in ancient Rome. Epictetus pinpointed what he believed was his principal purpose. It is something decision-makers would do well to memorise:

The chief task in life is simply this: to identify and separate matters so that I can say clearly to myself which are externals not under my control,

43

and which have to do with the choices I actually control. Where then do I look for good and evil? Not to uncontrollable externals, but within myself to the choices that are my own.

The Stoics used this distinction, between the external world and internal control, to form a measured perspective on how to lead a good life. For them, recognising what was external to their control helped develop internal stamina and resilience.

The lesson for thinkers of the future is to accept that life is like a complicated picture that is constantly changing over time. But just because so much is beyond our control, it need not make us feel helpless. Nor should we swing the other way by exaggerating the outer limits of our influence into a belief that we can shape everything. Instead, the ability to think the future requires a clear delineation of the *boundaries* of our agency. This, in turn, will guide the decisions we make and the actions we take.

In short, although Stoic philosophy is rooted in ancient thinking, it can be applied in any field or industry. Today's strategic advisers can take a leaf out of the Stoics' book to provide a top-quality model to decision-makers at the pinnacle of authority. At its core is the control/no control distinction: on the one hand, get your clients to understand the scale and nature of the stormy seas they face; and on the other, get them to work out the best possible chances of steering the ship to where they want to go. That way they will leverage their resources for maximum gain and minimal loss and avoid wasting anything on futile pursuits.

It's a common misconception that Stoicism is about indifference to external events, even to the point of ignoring the outside world altogether. This is what the term 'stoical' has come to refer to, and a 'stoic' is defined as someone who represses their feelings. But that's not what the Stoic philosophers intended, nor is it what we are suggesting when linking Stoic teachings to thinking the future. We have to engage with the world; we cannot ignore it. But it's easy to be overwhelmed by its complexity and uncertainty if we link each and every event to our own destiny, and that's what these philosophers understood.

Great thinkers of the future are aware of the limits of their actions. They try to keep emotion out of the process by calmly proceeding through analysis and by evaluating how the external world may shape their decisions, and then they plot out the best way they can influence the world through the overlap between the two circles in the Venn diagram.

The Expanding Overlap

The pace at which the world changes has accelerated enormously in recent years through a combination of greater interconnectedness between nations across the globe and technological advances, particularly in the field of communication. This means that the two circles in the diagram have far greater interaction with each other. Developments in the large circle of no control are invading the smaller circle of what lies within the control of organisations and individuals at an unprecedented rate. Equally, one ordinary citizen can more easily do something in their little circle that then captures the world's attention and causes a sensational change in the dynamic of the big circle, despite it being entirely beyond their control. That overlap, where the two circles influence each other, is becoming bigger and more crucial by the day.

Let's look at the big circle first. The foremost example is the coronavirus pandemic, the first case of which was reported on 31 December 2019. It affected people's lives regardless of whether they were infected by the virus or not. Lockdowns around the world happened very suddenly, but their consequences will be felt for years. Modern-day Stoics will have suffered the least mental fatigue and stress, focusing instead on sensible changes in behaviour to reduce the risk of catching the virus and implementing measures to survive financially amid all the disruptions.

An example in the realm of business is an industry increasingly vulnerable to factors beyond its control: tobacco. Cigarette executives can't stop the increasing regulations that ban smoking in public spaces, the higher excise taxes and the growing public awareness about the long-term health risks associated with smoking. Nor can they influence the changing weather patterns caused by climate change, bringing about potential droughts in regions that grow tobacco leaves.

However, they can control the proportion of their budget that they invest in the research and development of alternative products to add to their range. A recent innovation in the industry is the e-cigarette, but vaping – although less harmful than traditional smoking – is not considered safe by medical experts. A Stoical executive would admit that there was still room for improvement and keep the pressure on the research team to come up with even better substitutes.

Of course, the forces that the big circle imposes on the small circle aren't always gradual; they can come thick and fast. Amid the pandemic, the South African government banned the sale of alcohol and tobacco during the more dire stages of its national lockdown in an effort to fight the spread of Covid-19 and reduce the strain on the healthcare system (alcohol-related injuries normally take up a significant number of beds and other resources). The impact on the two industries was immediate, but thankfully for many the ban was short-lived. Smokers and drinkers are back to their old habits ... for the time being.

The same outside pressure applies to the coal, oil and gas industries. Climate change is upon us and, to remain inhabitable, the planet must move to renewable sources of energy. As a Stoic, you would not dispute the evidence on melting ice sheets, rising sea levels, higher seasonal temperatures and the growing frequency of extreme weather events. Rather, if you were advising these industries on their future, you would be asking them whether they are researching ways of capturing carbon emissions while also exploring the most economical alternatives to fossil fuels – initiatives that lie within their control.

We move on to the small circle influencing the large circle. In *Nineteen Eighty-Four*, author George Orwell talked of Big Brother watching you. Today, the internet and the proliferation of smartphones mean that several *billion* little brothers and sisters could be watching you.

In May 2020, Derek Chauvin, a white police officer in Minneapolis, knelt on George Floyd's neck for nearly nine and a half minutes in the street, eventually killing him. Floyd was a black man whom Chauvin had intended to arrest, and video footage of the incident sparked waves of Black Lives Matter protests around the world. In light of further deaths caused by the brutality of American police, the waves of Chauvin's actions are still breaking into the big circle of no control. It has thrown the validity of US law enforcement into question, with calls to defund the police.

Today, surveillance works both ways. The police have cameras, but so do the public. Perhaps the hideous death of George Floyd, who had pleaded to the officer that he could not breathe, will usher in a new age where history is re-evaluated from different perspectives. Rethinking the past may be as important as thinking the future.

In contrast to the violent choices police officers make during an arrest, Greta Thunberg's choice to skip school on Fridays to protest against climate change in Sweden was virtuous. By doing so, she ignited awareness of the issue across the globe. She is now a household name and has added a real bite to the environmental movement. Thunberg famously scolded political decision-makers with the words 'How dare you' at the 2019 UN Climate Action Summit. Her actions as an individual challenged the commitment of national leaders to save the planet for the next generation and exposed their hypocrisy in failing to do so.

The increasing overlap between the two circles has irreversibly widened the ambit of uncertainty we experience in our lives. It has forced every individual, business, charity and government department to appreciate the interconnectedness of each moving part in the two circles of our diagram. We live in a complex system where the flapping of a butterfly's wings can, with a single beat, change the game in the universe at large. Nowadays, it may be sharing a video from your smartphone that activates the butterfly effect.

Given how things can go exponential so quickly these days, it is increasingly foolish to invoke the law of unintended consequences by thoughtlessly putting a foot wrong. Stoicism helps us lower those odds by focusing on how we ought to engage with the future. When we establish the extent of our control, we are less likely to get distracted by things beyond it. We can think more carefully about the possible implications of our actions and how they might reverberate in the outside world.

The truth is that we don't control much, but it's better to understand this than live in a fool's paradise. A splash of Stoic tonic will wake us from the dreamy slumbers where desires shape our destiny and fears unsettle our fate. And if there's a lesson to be learnt from incautious heroes who ignore the wisdom of the Stoics, it's from the pens of history's greatest playwrights: tragedy awaits.

The Complexity of Being Oedipus

Tragedy has a long and winding history that stretches back to the first great tragedian, Aeschylus, born around 525 BCE. Although the word 'tragedy', as applied to drama, is thought to come from the word tragōidia, or 'goat-song', tragedies are really plays about humans, and specifically about how suffering is part of the human condition. The characters' actions cause unexpected calamity from which further action cannot save them. As Simon Critchley points out in *Tragedy, the Greeks and Us*: 'The overwhelming experience of tragedy is a disorientation expressed in one bewildered and frequently repeated question: What shall I do?'

Each tragic play we see may look different, but they all share a general theme or formula comprising several essential elements. Aristotle, our now familiar fox, distilled the ingredients to any good tragedy in his work *Poetics*. If it were a recipe, it would read a little like this:

1. Start with one protagonist – someone like yourself, but more fortunate in some way: smarter, better-looking or more powerful. However, said character also has a critical flaw, otherwise known as a *hamartia*, which they do not readily acknowledge.

2. Pierce the skin of the protagonist by having them commit a tragic deed – *pathos*. Be careful not to cut too deep; the tragic deed must be unintentional.

3. Rub salt into the wound by ensuring that the tragic deed is linked to the protagonist's critical flaw.

4. Heat up a reversal of fortune that the protagonist will experience. Make them suffer further complications associated with steps 2 and 3 to evoke pity and fear in the minds of your guests.

5. Sear the protagonist until they recognise their mistake. Then flip the protagonist over so that the character moves from ignorance to knowledge.

6. If you really want to make the dish special, perform the steps above to make it all seem inevitable – perhaps a fate dictated by the gods – yet apparently achieved by the protagonist exercising free will. The contradiction will create tension.

7. By the end, your dinner guests should have undergone *katharsis* – a

kind of pleasure that comes from experiencing various emotions associated with watching the protagonist's demise.

If done properly, this dish should keep for decades, centuries, even aeons.

One way the tragic recipe has been artfully presented across the ages is by presenting the protagonist with a prophecy foreshadowing their fate. Think of the witches in Shakespeare's *Macbeth*:

> Be lion-mettled, proud, and take no care
> Who chafes, who frets, or where conspirers are.
> Macbeth shall never vanquish'd be until
> Great Birnam Wood to high Dunsinane Hill
> Shall come against him.

Macbeth thinks it impossible for Birnam Wood to move, so he believes in his own indestructibility. But the wood does move, in the form of an army camouflaged with boughs from the trees of the forest.

And consider the Oracle of Delphi in Sophocles's *Oedipus Rex*:

> You are fated to couple with your mother, you will bring a breed of children into the light no man can bear to see – you will kill your father, the one who gave you life!

Oedipus immediately leaves what he thinks is his parental home upon hearing the oracle's prophecy, but he still ends up (as you will likely have guessed if you haven't read it) unknowingly killing his father and coupling with his mother.

Although Macbeth and Oedipus have their futures read out to them, each decision the protagonists make still seems to emanate from their own volition; or at least it appears so to them. And here's the rub: by trying to avoid the prophecy, they actually bring it about.

In *Myth and Tragedy in Ancient Greece*, eminent historians Jean-Pierre Vernant and Pierre Vidal-Naquet highlight how tragedies revolve around a relationship between fate and agency:

The true domain of tragedy lies in that border zone where human actions are hinged together with the divine powers, where – unknown to the agent – they derive their true meaning by becoming an integral part of an order that is beyond man and that eludes him.

Writers of tragedy dangle a stick of free will in front of their leading characters, but their future is literally scripted for them. It's this misbelief in the true scope of their control – the limits of their agency – which leads them down the fated path of their demise. And, despite forewarnings, the protagonists make the choices they do because they're blinded by their own perceived ability to carve out their destiny. Put simply, the likes of Macbeth and Oedipus could do with a tall glass of Stoic tonic.

The bottom line is that Stoics do not get to star in tragedies because the leading role will not suit them; they'd accept fate, not try to fight it. Stoicism teaches us to be aware of the limits to our control, and thereby functions as a check on our intentions. By contrast, tragedies can be considered cautionary tales for how things can go wrong if we try to extend the power of our influence beyond what reality warrants. They give us the opportunity to reflect on the actions of people who refuse to accept that some things are beyond their control. As such, it's tempting to dismiss them as tales about arrogance, but real life has no shortage of dire consequences for those who ignore their complicated relationship with the future and are swept up by a desire to take back control.

Unleashing Demons

In 2013, UK prime minister David Cameron made a long-awaited speech on Britain's membership of the European Union at Bloomberg's headquarters in London. He tried to balance what he saw as a need to reform the terms of the relationship with a reassertion of the importance of continuing to be a member. Following a well-considered argument for how he saw Britain's future, he concluded: 'That is why I am in favour of a referendum. I believe in confronting this issue – shaping it, leading the debate. Not simply hoping a difficult situation will go away.'

He then put forward a proposal that would be the crux of the Conservative Party manifesto for the next general election: 'And when we have negotiated that new settlement, we will give the British people a referendum with a very simple in-or-out choice to stay in the EU on these new terms; or come out altogether. It will be an in/out referendum.'

This was arguably one of the biggest moments in his premiership. Cameron's goal was to prevent his citizens' growing discontent with the European Union from boiling over to the point where the majority of people in the UK wanted out. He put his head on the block to settle an issue that had been simmering for decades. Somewhere in the wings, the witches were stirring the cauldron.

In 2015, the very year he won re-election, David Cameron was on his way to deliver another speech. Alongside him in the prime minister's official bulletproof Jaguar was Craig Oliver – his director of politics and communications – and a big red box containing official government papers. Cameron was running through reasons for holding the referendum. Oliver, playing the Socratic aide, asked him if he could see the case *against* it. Undoubtedly more candid in trusted company, Cameron replied: 'You could unleash demons of which ye know not.'

Oliver considered the phrase and googled it, thinking it either biblical or Shakespearean in origin, but he found nothing. It seemed to be Cameron's own. Oliver did, however, find a quote from the prophetic fool in Shakespeare's tragedy *King Lear*, which sums up the events that followed: 'Let go thy hold when a great wheel runs down the hill, lest it break thy neck with following it.'

Cameron's 'unleashing of demons' comment would prove prophetic in the tragic sense, because that's exactly what happened in his decision to hold a referendum. If he thought sense would prevail – as much as 'sense' exists in the world of politics – he was proven spectacularly wrong. Passions ran high, simmering tensions rose to the surface, and in the run-up to the 2016 Brexit Referendum, British politics ran out of control.

Cameron had let a giant wheel roll down a hill, and when he tried to hold it back, Boris Johnson – at the time mayor of London – and Nigel Farage, then leader of the UK Independence Party, jointly applied their shoulders to accelerate it. They played on England's North–South divide and exacerbated fears over illegal immigration. It paid off. Cameron lost the vote to stay and paid the personal political price.

As if he were being served up in the ancient Greek recipe for tragedy, Cameron delivered the very mechanism that would pave the way for his own undoing. He fulfilled the very fate he was trying to avoid: Brexit, as well as his own professional demise.

On the morning after the referendum, Cameron stood in front of 10 Downing Street and read out his intention to step down as prime minister. The analogy he chose would not have been lost on the Stoics: 'I will do everything I can as prime minister to steady the ship over the coming weeks and months, but I do not think it would be right for me to try to be the captain that steers our country to its next destination.'

This speech marked a moment of reckoning for Cameron, which, as Richard Sewell highlights in *The Vision of Tragedy*, is the moment when 'the conflict between man and his destiny assumes once more the ultimate magnitude'. It is the moment when the path you choose crosses the path that fate has in store for you. Reluctantly, you take the latter.

The decision to hold a referendum will be debated for years. Unlike tragedy in the theatre, where the fate of the protagonist is truly in the lap of the gods, tragedy in real life can result from misperceiving the reality in the big circle of no control to the extent that it destroys a significant portion of your own circle. This happened to Cameron.

While there are different sides to every debate and it's always easier to be smart in hindsight, a Stoic might have been more aware of the potential consequences of his own actions. Having been proved wrong, he would then accept that what's done is done. There is no place for 'if only'. Thinking the future is based on the world as it is, not the world as we want it to be. The only sensible question for analysts and UK citizens to ask today is: How do we navigate the sea of change caused by Brexit?

After all, that voyage has already begun and poses plenty of new challenges.

A Measure of Stoical Happiness

There's an old idiom from Greek mythology about being caught between Scylla and Charybdis, two immortal sea monsters who inhabited the Straits of Messina, the narrow channel between Sicily and the Italian mainland.

Scylla, described as a six-headed monster, presented herself as a shoal of hidden rocks that would cause ships to founder. Charybdis acted like a swirling whirlpool that could suck ships in. Because they were so close to one another, passing between them posed an inescapable risk – you could avoid one, but not both. It's the same as being 'caught between a rock and a hard place' or having to choose 'the lesser of two evils'. Homer's hero Odysseus was advised to guide his rowing boat closer to Scylla and lose a few rowers rather than risk his entire ship being swallowed by Charybdis. He complied with the advice and lost six men. Later, while stranded on a raft, he was swept back into the strait close to Charybdis. He managed to survive again, this time by hanging on to a fig tree growing on a rock above the monster's lair.

Stoics are often portrayed as people with a gloomy and withdrawn disposition. To counter that perception, we will present to you two giants who bore their misfortunes with Stoic pride. They successfully steered themselves between rocks and hard places and achieved a certain amount of happiness in doing so. One was John Milton, who composed exquisite poetry in the seventeenth century. The other was Ludwig van Beethoven, who composed exquisite music in the late eighteenth and early nineteenth centuries. During their respective lives, the first went blind and the second went almost completely deaf, thus losing the faculties most critical to their art. Yet they both coped well enough to continue working.

Milton wrote a famous sonnet known as 'On His Blindness'. In this poem, Milton reflects on his existence and discovers that God is not that interested in man's work or gifts. Rather, the Divine Being believes that people who happily 'bear his mild yoke' serve him best. The message is clear if you take your cue from the word 'mild': make do as best you can with whatever fate has in store for you, and whatever circumstances you were born into. You do not have to perform extraordinary feats to have a good life. The poem ends with the line: 'They also serve who only stand and wait'.

Stoics play the cards they are dealt. Milton went totally blind in his early forties, and for the rest of his life he dictated his verse and prose to amanuenses, or literary assistants, who acted as his scribes. *Paradise Lost* and *Paradise Regained* were two of his most popular works, but in his actual life he neither lost nor regained paradise when he went blind. He soldiered on with distinction.

Beethoven started to notice problems with his hearing in his late twenties, around 1798. He also experienced a constant ringing and buzzing in his ears, an affliction now known as tinnitus. As he wrote later to a friend: 'For two years I have avoided almost all social gatherings because it is impossible for me to say to people "I am deaf." If I belonged to any other profession, it would be easier, but in my profession, it is a frightful state.'

Beethoven's growing deafness did not prevent him from composing music. Indeed, all nine of his symphonies were performed for the first time from 1800 onwards, and his first set of string quartets was published in 1801. As his hearing deteriorated, he was forced to imagine what his masterpieces would sound like in a concert hall. At the same time, he found it more difficult to play the piano at concerts, which constituted a significant portion of his income in his younger years. Yet in his lifetime he was – and still is today – one of the most admired composers of all time. One music critic put it this way: 'He did what he did in the face of overwhelming difficulty.'

There are many similar stories of ordinary people beating huge odds to lead a fulfilling life. We come back to the two circles of control and no control: never be too despondent about what happens in the school of hard knocks because, more often than not, there are ways of ameliorating the impact of the blows. Being long-suffering does not exclude happiness. This all leads us to ask the following questions:

1. How often do you get emotionally consumed by matters beyond your control, such as the news or some drama on social media? Try separating the issues into what can affect you and what is irrelevant but interesting. Can you be a Stoic when hearing bad news that could have implications for your future? Can you concentrate on how you should react to the consequences as best as possible?

2. Draw our Venn diagram and fill it with things in life that are important to you but lie beyond your control, as well as the important features that you can control. Which of these things belong in the region of influence where the circles overlap? This is where the environment affects you, but where you can also affect your

environment. Does reflecting on these matters change your strategic outlook?

3. Have you ever done something that caused a chain of unexpected events to spiral out of your control? Did that action turn out to be beneficial beyond your wildest hopes, or did it unleash demons that still come back to haunt you? What lessons can you draw from the experience?

4. Consider your response to the coronavirus pandemic and its lockdowns. Did you waste a lot of time worrying about things beyond your control and languish at home? If, in the aftermath, you shift to a Stoic response and focus on the personal actions and feelings you can control, what will you do to improve your situation and that of others? Are there things you discovered about yourself during lockdown that will change the way you live in years to come?

5. Have you ever been caught been a rock and a hard place on some major issue affecting your life? Did you manage to choose the lesser of the two evils to minimise the damage?

Chapter 4

How to Re-perceive the World

*Don't go through life as a blinkered racehorse looking straight
in front of you. Take your blinkers off to see the future around you.*
Pierre Wack

Pierre Wack, the scenario-planning giant who fascinated all who met him,
made the opening quote to accentuate the need for peripheral vision. He
wanted us to capture the fringes of life because, as we have already said,
plotting out an unusual scenario in advance of it happening is a skill that
sets good futurists apart from the rest. Before examining his message in
detail, we would like to show that what we are proposing in this chapter is
something we have all done, every day, since we were very young. There is
nothing revolutionary in considering multiple possibilities and weighing
up the best options for meeting a challenge.

Most of us are born as foxes with a natural ability to manoeuvre under
pressure. Think back to when you were a child and your parents caught
you doing something wrong. You looked at their faces to see if they had
really caught you, and then you decided whether to tell the truth or a
porky-pie. That decision would depend on what you expected the response
to be, based on their mood, their facial expressions and your existing knowledge about your parents. In milliseconds, you made a judgement call and
gave your version of events with as much conviction as you could muster.
If their answer surprised you, you might have changed tactics, but whatever route you took had 'damage limitation' written all over it.

If you play chess, you learn soon enough that you need to plot your
opponent's possible moves before making the next one yourself. You need
to play different scenarios, assign intuitive probabilities to the range of
available moves and what your opponent may do in return, and only then
move your own piece. The trick to winning is to have a chain of moves up

57

your sleeve that your opponent does not anticipate and that will determine the end of the game in your favour.

A Blinkered Business Mind

If we are naturally dynamic thinkers, then how come hedgehog-like thinking starts intruding on our lives? The answer is simple: It all begins when thinking the future becomes 'group-thinking' the future and you feel pressured to conform. Companies and other organisations normally have hierarchical structures, where teamwork with a clear objective is essential for success. Accordingly, the model that has been around since *The Practice of Management* by Peter Drucker was published in 1954 has underlined the following qualities for a company to prosper: an overall vision defining the purpose of the company; a mission statement describing how the vision will be implemented; and key performance indicators against which to measure the performance of all employees, from the CEO to the front-line workers, in fulfilling the vision.

As we know from team sports like cricket, football and rugby, this approach can promote excellent results on the field of play. You need only look at the abundance of soccer trophies that Manchester United won under Alex Ferguson's firm leadership to see that singularity of purpose can lead to victory.

Nevertheless, everything begins to fall apart as you switch from the present to the future. Business leaders with a good earnings track record tend to build on successful strategies from previous years to determine the strategy for the future. They want to repeat their past successes. The planning team is there to draw up detailed financial projections flowing out of the strategy, and then come up with programmes to implement it. The planners seldom question whether the strategy is still valid despite changes in the market or operating environment. They are not paid to do so. Adam Grant, a professor in organisational psychology at the University of Pennsylvania, notes in his book *Originals* that managers 'focus too much on reasons to reject an idea and stick too closely to existing prototypes'. They reel off that old adage: 'If it ain't broke, don't fix it.' But what if the environment around 'it' is changing?

The rot starts here, because what worked in the past may not work in the future. Competitors may have come up with innovative products and ways to market them, consumer tastes may be moving in a different direction, technologies may be making your products or marketing methods obsolete, legislation may be creating new rules of the game in your industry, and the countries in which you operate may be about to experience a sharp change in their political or economic fortunes. Overarching all these factors are global phenomena such as wars, terrorism, waves of populism, trade conflicts, climate change and, of course, pandemics.

The trouble in many businesses is that pointing out what Al Gore called 'inconvenient truths' is usually not good for your career, and in particular your prospects of promotion and a higher salary. To earn more money – or perhaps to simply *continue* earning money – you must stay in line with conventional thinking. It all adds up to an incentive to hunker down with an array of obedient hedgehogs, even if you are a fox by nature.

Moreover, risk management is seen as an internal affair. Auditors and audit committees exist to ensure compliance with accounting, tax, safety and environmental regulations, and to check that staff are honest at work. When the financial solvency of a business is assessed (a legal responsibility assigned to the board of directors), it's usually done according to a short-term financial forecast. This forecast often presumes business as usual.

The result is that risk management very rarely covers the kinds of *external* risks that come with a constantly changing world. If it does, the risks will probably just get listed in a special document for the board to peruse. This is typically just an exercise in ticking the boxes. A fierce debate about change and adaptation would consume too much precious time in a crowded meeting agenda, so it simply doesn't happen. At the end of the day, giving directors a list of risks to manage is like splashing water on a stone, and will probably do nothing to align the decision-makers' picture of reality with reality itself.

A common substitute is for companies to hold annual strategic workshops with internationally renowned outside experts presenting the latest trends in the industry. The problem is that such functions are more of a social-bonding exercise than a space where the top brass allow participants to voice alternative views on the way forward. Furthermore, people usually need an ongoing process, involving a series of discussions, to enable them to think the future in a fundamentally different way.

Any experienced therapist would tell you that it takes more than one session with a patient to change their mind. The dialogue must be spread out over time. Once a year is simply not enough for companies.

The rigidity of thinking among senior executives, accompanied by a lack of questioning, means that top companies come and go like songs in the pop charts. If you look at the Dow Jones Industrial Average in the US and the Financial Times Stock Exchange 100 Index in the UK, the companies making up both indices are now very different to the ones in place fifty years ago. It prompts the question: Where will all the businesses currently topping the charts be in several years' time? Moreover, where will *you* end up if you're working for one of these companies and it's on its way out because it's too big and rigid to evolve?

This is a fitting introduction to scenario planning, which Pierre Wack liked to call the 'gentle art of re-perception'.

Taking the Blinkers Off

Wack was a beguiling individual because you could not classify him. He was a French oil executive but had regularly studied under Indian gurus. He liked the smell of incense to pervade his office so that he could see more clearly into the future. Most importantly, he absorbed the thinking of Herman Kahn, an American military analyst who pioneered the methodology of scenario planning in a book titled *On Thermonuclear War*, published in 1960.

The term 'scenario planning' came about through Kahn's friendships with Hollywood screenwriters who summarised their scripts into shorter scenarios for busy movie producers to read. This gave him an idea: Rather than forecasting the future, which is a relatively boring way of looking ahead, why not *explore* the future by writing stories about it? These narratives could both stimulate the mind and help formulate strategy.

Kahn's book painted in-depth scenarios of full-scale nuclear conflict and its potential outcomes. In doing so, he exposed the pitfalls of mutually assured destruction, a military policy which, very basically, argues that if you nuke me, I'll nuke you and we'll both be annihilated, so having a nuclear arsenal means that we're forced to be sensible and not nuke each

one another at the same time. The ideas are incompatible, so you can dismiss that scenario, leaving one quadrant in the matrix blank.

The other approach is to bundle all the key uncertainties together so that positive outcomes in one direction create an upside scenario, and negative outcomes in the other direction create a downside scenario. This is sometimes called the binary model of scenario planning. The assumption here is that the uncertainties all reinforce one another in either direction. It's a blunter use of scenarios than the technique we have just shown you, and it takes less account of the potential nuance and complexity in the real world. However, it can be a powerful way of showing the stark contrast between two possible paths into the future.

In the career example, you might list the degree, financial support, work experience, mentorship and the availability of job opportunities as key uncertainties. Each of these things affects your ability to change your career, and if you get positive outcomes in all of them, then you get the 'good' future. If they remain out of your reach in a combined negative outcome, then you get the 'bad' future and return to your old job – if it is still there. The two scenarios offer an 'either/or' picture of the future, similar to consulting the Delphic Oracle on a quick yes/no question.

This is not the end of the process. Thinking the future like a fox demands that you consider your options and risks in light of the scenarios and make decisions that are then effectively implemented via action. These steps must lie within your circle of control. The worst-case scenario of the career exercise might be a depressing one, but by sketching it before the start of the career-change journey, you are able to face the facts and mitigate the risks.

You could, for example, create an emergency savings account and keep in touch with old colleagues who could help with employment options in your previous industry. Similarly, although the best-case scenario is probably what you had in mind from the start, seeing it on paper might motivate you to focus on your studies (a factor that is within your control), while also maintaining a healthy relationship with your partner and helping them in their career (factors that you can't fully control, but which you can influence).

Forward into the Future

We shall now give you some bigger-picture examples of both approaches using our own views of the future. The first is a climate-change exercise that looks at the future of the world beyond 2021, paying special attention to the natural environment. One rule of the game is that the challenge of climate change is so huge that it can *only* be tackled by nations on a co-operative basis. They must abandon rampant nationalism in favour of solving this collective threat.

A second rule is that the world must be enjoying a sufficient level of economic prosperity across all its nations to afford the measures required to create a greener economy. Accordingly, the degree of inequality between nations must diminish in the process of making the planet sustainable in the long run.

There are three key uncertainties: Will nations come out of the pandemic united or disunited in promoting economic recovery? Will the Paris Agreement to combat climate change be taken seriously enough to achieve measurable results in reducing carbon emissions? Finally, what will the actual rate of climate change be? The first two uncertainties have been identified as crucial because they influence the third one, and thus we have used them to produce the matrix shown below. The horizontal axis moves from 'Green Apathy' on the left to 'Green Commitment' on the right. The vertical axis has 'Global Unity' at the top and 'Global Disunity' at the bottom.

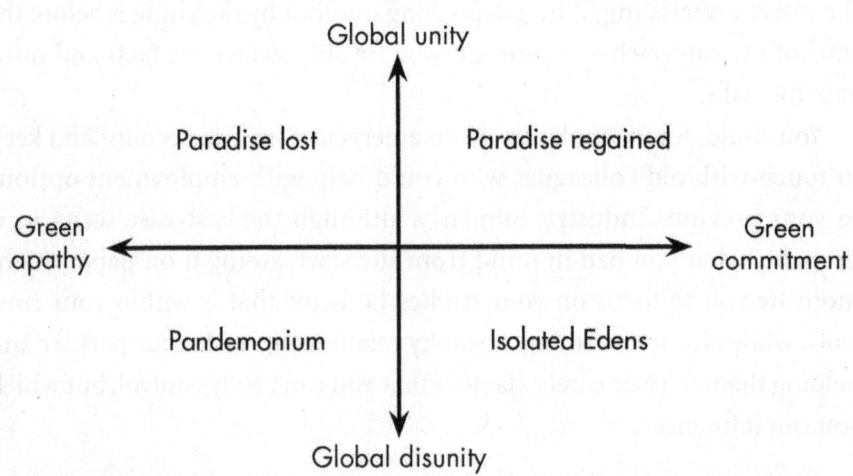

These axes combine to give the scenarios shown, and we've named them with a nod to the poetry of John Milton. The most positive one is 'Paradise Regained', on the top right of the matrix. This is where genuine progress is made, because the Paris Agreement sets measurable targets that nations are legally obligated to meet, and the global economy recovers sufficiently from the pandemic for nations generally to afford to meet those targets.

In contrast, 'Paradise Lost' at the top left of the matrix is where, as Greta Thunberg observed in the last chapter, hypocrisy prevails among the rich nations, with plenty of rhetoric but no significant action, and this attitude is adopted by the rest of the world as a consequence.

In the bottom right-hand quadrant, we have 'Isolated Edens': a few nations break ranks and seek to preserve their own environments as best they can. Scandinavian countries will be among those conservation nations, as they tend to put the pursuit of happiness ahead of the pursuit of economic success.

The last scenario, on the bottom left, is dramatically called 'Pandemonium', because without global commitment or sufficient funding, climate change kicks in with such a vengeance that chaos reigns around the world, with no clear international strategy to counter it. Millions of people try to escape from regions that become uninhabitable because of rising sea levels, extreme weather and soaring temperatures.

In the next chapter, we will be identifying the flags to watch in order to see which of these four scenarios is most likely to happen. Meanwhile, let's turn to an example of the binary, either/or approach to scenarios.

As an illustration, we have chosen the possible paths that South Africa can take out of the coronavirus pandemic. The first rule of the game is that, to safeguard the open democracy that South Africa became in 1994, attention must now switch to economic transformation that opens up economic opportunities for all citizens.

The second rule is that South Africa right now stands at an economic crossroads after years of corruption and state capture, combined with the disruptive impact of Covid-19. The coffers are virtually empty, and this is unlikely to change any time soon. We are at a tipping point where the path we take in the immediate future could define our future for decades.

The third rule is that any initiative to save the South African economy must be bottom-up as well as top-down, driven by communities, municipalities, provinces and the private sector in the first sense, and driven by the government in the second sense. It is only by working together as a team that we will end up with an economy that uplifts everyone.

The fourth rule only came into effect in this century: automation has fundamentally changed the nature of work, and robotics and artificial intelligence are now a standard part of mass-production systems. In addition, big business is no longer the major creator of jobs anywhere in the world. It has been replaced by small and micro business.

According to a recent report by the Small Business Administration based in America, small companies account for 64 per cent of new jobs created there. To reduce South Africa's hideous unemployment rate, any initiative will have to stimulate a new entrepreneurial wave across the entire nation. The focus must be on creating millions of new enterprises that, in turn, will create millions of jobs.

There are plenty of key uncertainties and all are considered crucial. Will future government policies be based on pragmatism instead of ideology in terms of reshaping the economy and widening the ownership of land? Will stimulating an entrepreneurial revolution be a key part of this policy? Will corruption be rooted out and dealt with in a way that ensures that clean and honest practices become the norm in both the public and private sectors? Will government prioritise improvements in physical infrastructure, health delivery and the education system to provide the platform for ordinary citizens to lead better lives? Will we accept the challenge of creating a greener economy? A 'yes' to these questions is part and parcel of a positive outcome. A 'no' leads to the negative outcome.

One final key uncertainty goes back to the global climate-change exercise described before this one. Whichever of the four environmental scenarios materialises will significantly affect South Africa's fortunes along with those of every other country in the world.

With these key uncertainties, and consistent with our rules of the game, there are two scenarios. The first one we call 'People's Economy', to convey the message that the work achieved by Nelson Mandela and others, before and after the dawn of South Africa's democracy, constitutes unfinished business. In this sequel to the watershed event that was the 1994 general election, the country now achieves economic freedom for all as a necessary complement to political freedom. The government creates an inclusive economy with a new generation of young entrepreneurs at the helm. At the same time, the world economy recovers and remains open for business, with rich countries providing poorer countries with enough assistance to start catching up. Meanwhile, humanity's collective carbon footprint is reduced in an effective manner.

The second scenario we call 'Cautionary Tale'. Here, South Africa experiences rising popular anger, caused by an economy that is stagnant, exclusive and cursed by a dismally high unemployment rate. This leads to further disunity and widespread violence with a possible end point of total anarchy in the chain of causation.

However, as the title of this scenario suggests, we think the odds of this happening are low – for now. It will emerge from the background if South Africans from all corners of society do not heed the rules of the game we mentioned earlier – particularly the one about working together as a team. Again, we will be listing the flags to watch in the next chapter, so that you can assess the odds on the two scenarios as the future unfolds.

All in all, we are indebted to Pierre Wack for his contribution to our model of thinking the future. We have given you a personal, global and national example of his methodology. Wack was considered unconventional in the business world, but he had charisma and charm as well. During his lifetime he assembled a group of fellow futurists around him, and these remarkable people turned thinking the future into a passion for us lesser mortals. Wack wrote two seminal articles for the *Harvard Business Review* in 1985: 'Scenarios: Uncharted Waters Ahead' and 'Scenarios: Shooting the Rapids'. We suggest you read them both.

Wack's favourite expression was that it was much better to be vaguely right than precisely wrong when thinking the future. He himself offered this description about his purpose in life: 'I had the feeling of hunting in a pack of wolves, being the eyes of the pack, and sending signals back to the rest.' Foxes fall into the same category. Therefore, we are putting ourselves in his shoes – or paws – by asking the following questions:

1. What does your microcosm, or mental model, of the world around you look like? Is your microcosm so strongly held that it inhibits you from re-perceiving the world by considering scenarios incompatible with your microcosm?
2. Given that business and other team activities propel us in the direction of conformist groupthink practices, will you be prepared to have conversations with colleagues about scenarios that might upset them because they raise uncomfortable possibilities? In answering this question, remember that the most valuable scenarios cover possible tipping points that can turn the future upside down.
3. Try imagining different scenarios of where you will be in ten years' time. Start by figuring out the rules of the game that are common to all your futures and give particular attention to the rules of winning or succeeding at the game. Next, make a short list of key uncertainties that could change your life and select two crucial uncertainties that are likely to shape your future, depending on whether they have positive or negative outcomes. Plot these two uncertainties as a pair of intersecting axes, as we have demonstrated. Describe personal scenarios for each of the four quadrants and give them gripping titles. What do they look like, and what are you going to do about the opportunities and threats they offer?
4. Supposing you want to influence other people's thinking and behaviour by using this model, how would you go about doing so? Do you agree that you should write the narrative of each scenario like a movie script, as we recommend, to engage their curiosity? How else might you grab their attention?
5. Do you think that climate change is currently the biggest threat to our existence on this planet? If not, what is? On the other hand, what gives you the most hope that later generations will have a better quality of life than you do? Is there any way you can help?

It is apt to close this chapter with a quote from former US president Theodore Roosevelt: 'Nine-tenths of wisdom consists in being wise in time.' Nobody understood that better than Pierre Wack.

Chapter 5

Flagging the Future

The aim of argument, or of discussion,
should not be victory but progress.
Karl Popper

Like good futurists, we all talk about the weather with one another. It's considered banal, but it happens everywhere. Here is a sample:

'Look how dark those clouds are. I think it's going to rain today.'

'Yeah, my weather app said there was a good chance of rain.'

'We better take our umbrellas then.'

An analysis of the conversation would state that the first comment is a personal opinion that the odds for rain are more than 50:50, based on the sighting of dark clouds, which are a familiar sign. The second comment backs up the opinion with a sophisticated assessment from a source with access to a much larger data bank. The third comment is a suggestion to action following reassurance that the hunch was probably right.

In terms of the Stoic model we are advocating in this book, the two participants examine what they don't control (the weather) before moving on to what they do control (taking umbrellas). But there is more to it than that. The first person identified the dark clouds as a sign or *flag* that has a reliable causal connection to the scenario of rain, and then linked that flag to a probability (i.e., rain today is highly probable).

What we want to show you in this chapter is that using flags as a sign of things to come allows you to attach intuitive probabilities, which have a degree of reasoning behind them, to the scenarios of interest. Merely proposing scenarios – it will rain today or it will not – is of little use to anyone; you can say that about the weather every day, and it certainly won't lead to any action without a statement about the odds.

These odds may change as the day proceeds and the clouds change shape and colour. Providing scenarios on all eventualities without giving an opinion on the one most likely to occur is devoid of validity. It cannot be proven true or false by what actually happens.

Karl Popper, an Austrian-British philosopher and social commentator upon whose giant shoulders we stand in this chapter, would have confirmed this. But he would have done so in a slightly different and possibly more elegant way. One of the quotes that confirmed Popper's reputation as a brilliant philosopher of the sciences is as follows: 'In so far as a scientific statement speaks about reality, it must be falsifiable; and in so far as it is not falsifiable, it does not speak about reality.' A statement is considered falsifiable if you can prove it false by observation. 'It will rain today' is falsifiable because if it doesn't rain, we know it was false.

Pierre Wack used to emphasise that any scenario in conflict with the stated rules of the game should be discarded as impossible – period. However, if that future then materialised, it would mean that you got the rules of the game wrong, and that your assertion regarding the rules of the game had been falsified. The scenario-planning model therefore passes Popper's test as a method that can be applied to the real world around us.

In our climate-change exercise, one of our unstated rules of the game is that the crisis is being caused by large-scale human activity, such as the burning of fossil fuels for energy. However, denialists argue that global warming is not linked to human carbon emissions, but that it is part of a cycle and that the world will start cooling down again at some point in the future, irrespective of what humanity does to reduce emissions. If the world does start cooling down with no reduction in emissions, then the entire basis of the last chapter's four environmental scenarios will have been falsified. We obviously don't think that will be the case, but the very fact that the denialist rule can be entertained would get Popper's thumbs-up that our methodology can be applied to the real world.

Capturing an Outlier

Turning from a relatively harmless event like rain to one of the deadliest tragedies in world history, we want to show how identifying and responding to flags has saved people's lives. On 26 December 2004, a 9.1 magnitude earthquake occurred in the Indian Ocean with an epicentre located 160 kilometres off the western coast of northern Sumatra. It was the third largest earthquake ever recorded, and it lasted between eight and ten minutes, the longest duration ever observed. It triggered a series of tsunamis that struck the coastlines of countries all around the Indian Ocean as far as the east coast of Africa, killing 227 898 people in fourteen countries.

Ten-year-old Tilly Smith was holidaying with her parents at a hotel in Phuket on the day of the tsunami. In a geography lesson at school two weeks earlier, Tilly had learnt that the signs of an imminent tsunami were an abnormal ebbing of the tide, revealing much more of the beach than usual, and frothing bubbles on the surface of the sea. On the beach in Phuket that day, Tilly noticed both of these flags and alerted her parents to their significance. Her parents warned the other beachgoers and the staff at their hotel, and the beach was evacuated before the tsunami hit the shore.

The point of this remarkable story is that thinking the future in an intelligent way reduces the number of events that come out of the blue and really shock you. You might not be able to stop the event from happening, but you can avoid being blindsided by it. Equally, some of the most valuable futures thinking anticipates life-changing events and unusual turning points leading to futures that do not resemble the past. One doesn't normally think about the possibility of tsunamis while lying on the beach, but when the flags of one popped up, Tilly perceived them and realised that the probability of a tsunami scenario had changed from highly unlikely to virtually certain.

The other crucial takeaway is that Tilly and her parents showed foxy agility in spreading the message of the tsunami scenario they'd envisioned to those nearby and, most notably, to the hotel staff, who had the capacity to take more widespread action. Hedgehogs, meanwhile, would have been unable to cope because they would not have envisaged the crisis in the first place. Their minds tend to be closed off to the completely unexpected.

The Importance of Flags

Tilly's accurate flagging of the tsunami serves as a suitable introduction to Karl Popper's highly perceptive 1966 essay titled 'Of Clouds and Clocks:

An Approach to the Problem of Rationality and the Freedom of Man'. Popper saw things in the world as existing on a spectrum from completely disorganised at one extremity to highly organised on the other. Clouds – on the left of the spectrum – represented physical systems that, like gases, were irregular, disorderly and unpredictable. Clocks, on the right, were physical systems that were regular, orderly and highly predictable. He put seasonal weather patterns towards the right end of the spectrum as somewhat-reliable clocks, and puppies further left than old dogs because they hadn't been trained yet and were less reliable and consistent in their behaviour. He stated that the predictable movements of the planets in our solar system made them clocks, whereas individual gnats, flying in a cluster, would be classified as clouds because of their irregular movements inside the cluster.

He went on to criticise the proposition of physical determinism, which argues that all phenomena operate as part of a predictable system, and it is only our ignorance of some elements in the chain of cause and effect that forces us to see certain things as random or disorganised. This belief had dominated scientific thinking from Isaac Newton onwards, but Popper called it a nightmare in that it portrayed the whole world as a huge auto-maton with us as the cogwheels. Moreover, he cruelly added that the term 'cogwheel' would also apply to the physicists who believed in the theory.

Equally, he thought that the opposite belief, that all clocks are clouds and the world is fundamentally random, was just as unsupportable. He referred to the gnats again in his counterargument, saying that as a cluster they predictably stuck together while being disorderly at the individual level. Thus, he claimed that the world is a hybrid of clouds and clocks. It is neither totally chaotic nor totally organised.

The predictability and unpredictability of the universe is why you need flags as tools to negotiate the future. The rules of the game will stay the same, while the key uncertainties will drive the future in one direction or another. The flags are the signs along the way indicating the direction in which the key uncertainties are taking you and, therefore, which scenario is coming into play and which is fading into the background.

In terms of our scenario matrix of the last chapter, they provide an ongoing assessment of whether you are moving up or down the vertical axis and whether you are moving to the right or left on the horizontal axis.

By combining those two assessments, you can pinpoint the quadrant where your future might currently be located.

Flags can even influence the outcomes described by the scenarios, like a crowd at a soccer match. People react to signs of change, and that might help push the change in the same direction, cause it to slow down or perhaps turn it around. If the future concerned is within your control or influence, then the flags might indicate areas where you could take action to prevent the key uncertainties from developing in a negative direction.

North Korea's nuclear missile strategy is a key uncertainty in any range of scenarios examining the future stability of the Far East. A flag to watch here is North Korea's relationship with America. An increase or decrease in tensions between the two countries will affect the state of military readiness that North Korea maintains. This, in turn, will raise or lower the prospect of a regional conflict, particularly between North and South Korea.

Another flag is the level of international economic sanctions being imposed on North Korea, and whether they are being heightened or reduced. This will give an indication of how desperate the regime is to either reach a settlement on denuclearisation or ramp the programme up further.

A third flag is the number of missile tests North Korea chooses to conduct and where those missiles land. In the same way that asking the right questions is a key to thinking the future effectively, choosing the right flags to watch adds huge value in providing ongoing answers to these questions.

Let us give another example. The rate of climate change probably figures as a key uncertainty in scenarios appertaining to the future of the coal-mining and oil industries. It probably also features in economic scenarios for California in the US and New South Wales in Australia, because of the impact that forest fires and intense rainfall have already had on human activities in both states.

As the annual statistics flow in to reveal whether the rate of climate change is quicker or slower than expected, the difference between the actual and anticipated figures will constitute a flag. It will indicate whether the call to phase out fossil fuels will intensify or diminish, and it will be useful in assessing the new normal as to the frequency of fires and floods in California and parts of Australia. If the flag is red, one-in-a-century events may turn into one-in-a-decade episodes demanding a complete rethink in risk-management strategies.

Sometimes a flag is identified as a game-changer before any key uncertainties have been formulated or scenarios written. It is a prequel rather than a sequel to the exercise. A flag of this sort is so fresh and powerful that it cannot be ignored, and on these occasions the scenario-planning process has to be reversed: scenarios are extrapolated from the flag, as opposed to the flags being used to assess which of the anticipated scenarios is coming into being. Should the flag be a new but stable trend, it may later be converted into a rule of the game to act as the basis for a new set of scenarios. Alternatively, if it is a highly unpredictable phenomenon, it can evolve into a key uncertainty from which different scenario narratives will flow.

A great example of powerful flags changing our view of the future occurred in January 2021, when Amazon and SpaceX found themselves in a battle over outer space. SpaceX wanted to reduce the orbit altitude of some of the satellites in its Starlink constellation to increase connection speeds. However, Amazon responded by saying it was working on its own satellite system for Project Kuiper, and the planned reduction in altitude by SpaceX could endanger the safety of its future satellites in and around the same orbit. Each company accused the other of trying to sabotage their respective satellite internet plans.

We call this new flag 'crowded space'. At present, there is only one law governing outer space: the 1967 Outer Space Treaty, which has been ratified by 111 UN member states, including the United States, the UK and Russia. It establishes the principle that space is free for exploration and use by all nations, but no nation may claim sovereignty over outer space or any celestial body.

With all the activity now taking place in space, more laws will no doubt be in the offing, particularly since private companies are now starting to argue about their share of space. The flag also pinpoints our dependence on satellite systems to communicate with one another. What would happen if the internet went down worldwide because two satellites crashed and the resulting debris caused widespread damage to crucial components of our international communication network?

This scenario of cascading collisions between objects in low earth orbit was proposed by NASA scientist Donald J. Kessler in 1978, and it's known as the Kessler syndrome. You can see a depiction of it in the 2013 film *Gravity*, which explores the fate of an astronaut stranded in space after high-speed debris destroys a space shuttle in mid-orbit.

We currently feel that the crowded space flag will lead to a whole new raft of international legislation governing the use of space, and that this process will not be without its challenges for international relations. It would be wise to start playing scenarios on that eventuality now.

Separating Signals from Noise

In the last chapter we advised that you plan no more than four scenarios per exercise, to keep things simple and focused. For the same reason, we feel that the number of flags should be five or fewer for each scenario. The reason is that flags have to be closely monitored on a regular basis, and too many will prevent you from keeping track of all the relevant information as it becomes available. You must be able to separate the signals from the noise, and that requires time and concentration.

Japan's surprise attack on Pearl Harbor in December 1941 demonstrates this point clearly. As Roberta Wohlstetter said in her 1962 book *Pearl Harbor: Warning and Decision*:

It is much easier *after* the event to sort the relevant from the irrelevant signals. After the event, of course, a signal is always crystal clear; we can see now what disaster it was signalling, since the disaster has occurred. But before the event it is obscure and pregnant with conflicting meanings. It comes to the observer imbedded in an atmosphere of 'noise,' i.e. in the company of all sorts of information that is useless and irrelevant for predicting the particular disaster ... In short, we failed to anticipate Pearl Harbor not for want of the relevant materials, but because of a plethora of irrelevant ones.

Too many flags spoil the intelligence. An additional problem is focusing on the *wrong* flags, due to a failure to interrogate your assumptions and conventions, and the ways in which they might be skewing your view of the risks and uncertainties you face. A recent example comes from a report released in December 2020 on the deadliest terrorist attack in New Zealand's history.

On 15 March 2019, a white supremacist opened fire on two mosques in Christchurch during Friday prayers. He killed fifty-one worshippers and injured forty-nine others. The report found that intelligence officials had focused disproportionately on Islamic fundamentalism rather than threats posed by other extremist ideologies. In other words, they were distracted from the real flag, or even unaware of it, because they concentrated on the conventional flags in the field under scrutiny.

On 6 January 2021, we had a third example of an intelligence agency failing to spot the flags in advance – or at least failing to take them seriously. Capitol Hill, the US seat of government, was stormed by a mob of Donald Trump supporters attempting to prevent Congress from formalising Joe Biden's victory in the presidential elections.

Besides an unusual delay in getting law enforcement troops to the scene, it has become apparent that, in the weeks leading up to the invasion, there was plenty of evidence that right-wing extremists who'd rejected the election result would pose a threat on this day. Just like in New Zealand, no key uncertainties, scenarios or flags around the event were meaningfully explored in advance because the intelligence experts did not recognise – or, worse still, didn't want to recognise – their significance.

Consequently, the practice of separating signals from noise has two elements to it: do not spread your attention across too many flags; and be on the alert for significant flags that may contradict your existing assumptions about what to watch. The latter demands an enquiring mind, which is why we said in the opening chapter that there should be more foxes in intelligence agencies.

Assigning Probabilities

The other issue we wish to address is the *nature* of the probabilities you give to the different scenarios. As we've said before, one of the worst traps to fall into in thinking the future is to be too precise. In scientific experiments, you can repeat experiments to get a pattern of results that then gives you a fairly accurate estimate of the chances of each outcome. In contrast, the future only happens once; you can't replay life over and over again to test the probability of a scenario becoming reality. You must assess that probability from the present, which is normally unique in itself.

The first thing to bear in mind is that probabilities generally need to be intuitive, not calculated through any mathematical formula. However, the flags give you a sense of where things are headed, so it is not pure guess-work either. We have to find a compromise between assertion and doubt, and we can do that with an expression of probability.

There are two ways of depicting this. The first is to keep to words rather than quote figures: a 0 to 10 per cent probability is 'highly unlikely'; 10 to 30 per cent is 'unlikely'; 30 to 50 per cent is 'possible'; 50 to 70 per cent is 'probable'; 70 to 90 per cent is 'highly probable'; and 90 to 100 per cent is 'virtually certain'.

The second option is to quote percentages, but stick to the tens: 0 per cent, 10 per cent, 20 per cent and so forth. Remember, though, that with a suite of scenarios the total must add up to 100 per cent. If you have just two scenarios, one could have a probability of 70 per cent, in which case the other would be 30 per cent likely. If you have four scenarios, there might be a 50/30/10/10 split. The essential thing to note is that you have to adjust the probabilities of the scenarios according to the information you get from the flags attached to them. By comparing the current probabilities with the previous set, you will get a sense of direction in your thinking – whether you are becoming more or less optimistic. Of course, the time horizon of the scenarios must be held in mind along with the probabilities.

Take the way we are all trying to figure out when life will return to some kind of stability after the Covid-19 pandemic. There are two scenarios in play for 2022 as vaccination programmes proceed. The first is that the virus will be controlled to the point that new infections are minimal. Life will settle into a new normal.

The second scenario is that we have more waves of infection caused by different strains, and infection rates remain stubbornly high. Restrictions of one kind or another continue. Not even the experts can tell you with much certainty which scenario will materialise, but they can offer you odds.

And you can estimate them for yourself by collecting the latest data and following the news. You can also discuss the scenarios with your family and friends to ascertain their views and whether they are getting more optimistic or pessimistic as each week passes.

There's an argument often given in favour of being more precise than we have recommended. Once you have plotted a scenario or possible future, you can obtain a lot of statistical data for similar circumstances. This can yield a more exact probability of the scenario happening, based on how many times it happened under the same conditions in the past. This method works if you are looking at, say, the chances of being involved in a road accident, being a victim of crime, catching a nasty disease or winning the lottery. For instance, an urban study might show that if you walk down a particular street alone after 8 p.m., you are 50 per cent more likely to be mugged or assaulted than in the middle of the day.

A gambler at the races would also want accurate odds before placing their bet. In horse racing, these odds are calculated using a comparison of the horses' past performances, However, you cannot get around the fact that scenarios about real life are more complicated than a horse race. Although they do share the aspect of outsiders occasionally winning, you can't generate those sorts of odds about life in general, which is why it's better to quote probabilities either in word form or rounded-up percentages.

We think that medical doctors would agree with us. When they diagnose an injury or disease that could have serious consequences for your health, they will offer a range of interventions as well as some idea of the probabilities of success or failure. But that prognosis will be couched in cautious language.

Overall, the problem with statistics in futures thinking is that, for the majority of professional scenario work, the world has changed to the extent that the logic behind each scenario comprises a set of uniquely new factors for which no statistics exist. The future may resemble the past in some respects and differ in others, but it is the *differences* that you are trying to capture.

As the probability of a scenario increases, it may be worth looking out for sub-flags that indicate an even greater chance that the scenario is about to become reality. In the storming of Capitol Hill in January 2021, Donald

Trump's refusal to accept the election results was a sub-flag, as was his incendiary speech on the day. Those close to him added to the incitement to violence, with lawyer Rudy Giuliani calling for a 'trial by combat'. None of the words spoken were an explicit order to invade Congress, but any scenario planner worth their salt would have come up with a narrative in which a pro-Trump protest march could lead to an invasion of the buildings – particularly in light of their meagre protection at the time. Those in charge of the troops and police, however, did nothing until after the violence erupted.

We'll make one last point before moving back to the scenarios of the last chapter and attaching a list of flags to them. Humans have a natural tendency to give more than a fair share of credibility to scenarios that reflect their desires (you'll learn more about this tension between passion and reason in the next chapter). Flags are there to prick the emotional bubble and improve our consciousness of what is likely to happen, even though it may not be in our interest for it to happen. As you have already gleaned from this book, Stoics are equipped to handle both the good with the bad in the circle beyond their control by optimising the contents of the circle within their control. Flags, especially red flags, can bring you down to earth with a bump, but you'll end up in a happier place than if you rode the tide of emotion only to be marooned in a sea of dreams.

A flag that rises very suddenly can often be alarming or exciting enough to penetrate our emotional bubbles, regardless of the impact it signifies. The slow ascent of the flag of climate change sadly means that it is ignored by many political and other leaders accustomed to responding only to sudden threats. Fight-or-flight is ingrained in our biology. Moreover, if a flag is remote from our senses – like melting ice caps in the Arctic and Antarctic – it is easy for us to fail to grasp its significance and ignore it altogether. As such, the closer we are to a flag, the greater our chances of recognising it for what it is.

The Flags for Earth and South Africa in the 2020s

We shall now return to our climate change and South African scenario exercises and give you a list of flags to watch for each of them. For ease of reference, here is the second matrix of the previous chapter again:

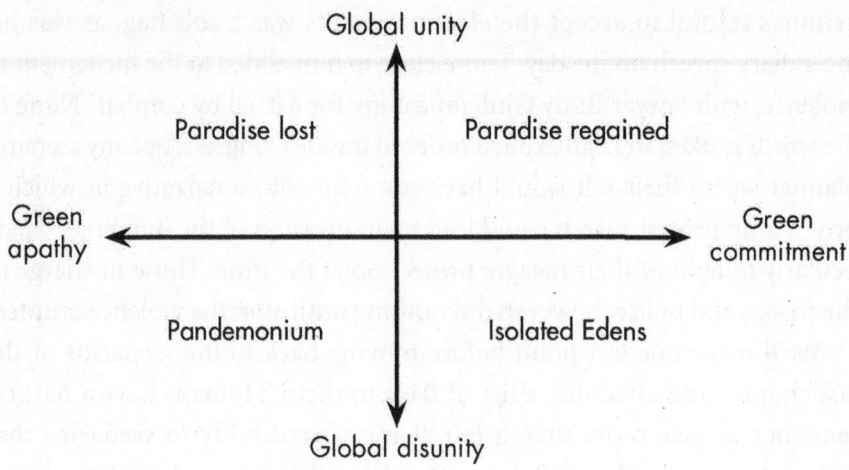

For the future of life on earth, the first and most obvious flag to watch is the relationship between the two largest carbon emitters in the world: the US and China. If they decide to get along with each other as best they can, they could jointly make the biggest dent in emissions and seek to bring the rest of the world on board by citing climate change as humanity's worst threat in this century. Their Green Commitment will be a powerful force in driving the world towards Paradise Regained.

If they remain amicable but neither is interested in putting the long-term sustainability of the planet ahead of short-term economic goals, then not only will they fail to make that critical reduction in emissions, but their Green Apathy will be shared by other nations. A move towards Paradise Lost will be on the cards, but a few nations might do what they can to form Isolated Edens. In the worst-case outcome of this flag, China and America descend from being strategic competitors into strategic enemies, climate change runs rampant, and Pandemonium ensues.

The second flag concerns the nature of the Paris Agreement and its ability to enforce Green Commitment. Paradise Regained is more likely to happen if the agreement becomes binding and all nations are compelled to attain specific targets for reducing their carbon emissions by a specific date, or face penalties if they do not do so. Harsh as it sounds, there is no other way to achieve the necessary level of commitment to eliminate the threat. If the penalties for non-compliance aren't harsh enough, we will move towards the less hopeful outcome of Isolated Edens. And if the Paris Agreement remains a voluntary affair, with plenty of pledges but little action, then Paradise Lost increases in probability.

The third flag is the capacity of technological advances to jump-start the move towards Green Commitment. If we don't have clean, sustainable and relatively cheap technologies to replace all the ones that are bad for our environment, then there will be nothing for a green economy to function on. In this respect, it is important to consider the entire carbon footprint of any innovation, including its complete supply chain and sources of energy.

For example, several nations have stated that they want to make a complete switch to electric vehicles by the 2030s, but how is the additional electricity going to be generated for the vehicles themselves? And what level of pollution will be emitted in building all the new infrastructure required to support the movement and maintenance of electric vehicles? Nobody has yet spelt out the details.

If technological advances for a greener economy do not actually produce the intended cuts in carbon emissions, then they will increase rather than decrease the probability of Paradise Lost and Pandemonium. If technological innovation is successful but not shared between nations, we are looking at Isolated Edens.

A fourth flag arises from a statistic in the 2020 UN *Emissions Gap Report*: the world's wealthiest 1 per cent of the population account for more than twice the carbon emissions of the poorest 50 per cent. This means that the rich need to change their selfish lifestyles. Private jets, air-conditioned mansions and fast cars will only continue to make matters worse. Society also needs to change its perspective on wealth so that materialistic consumption is no longer flaunted and admired. Other than enforcement by law, or the naming and shaming of individuals who exceed a reasonable carbon footprint, the only way to ensure this flag has positive momentum is to celebrate those people making lifestyle changes that render our planet more sustainable in the longer run. Otherwise, Paradise Regained will remain a dream.

The fifth flag revolves around building the capacity to monitor the results of all the actions taken by individual nations and their overall alignment with carbon-emission targets. If progress on the climate crisis can't be properly measured, then the experts and decision-makers lose the ability to assess and manage the problem. Nobody will really care that much until they are being directly affected by the increasing frequency of extreme weather events, rising sea levels, hotter temperatures and more widespread fires. This is the principal flag differentiating the pair of scenarios offered by Green Commitment on the right of our matrix from those arising out of Green Apathy on the left.

The Pandemonium scenario has some very dramatic additional flags that accompany it. If the rate of climate change turns out to be much faster than expected, then the number of climate refugees will skyrocket. Coastal cities will be put at risk by rising sea levels and bigger storms. The nations least affected by climate change will close their borders completely. International trade and travel will be disrupted more than was the case in the coronavirus pandemic. The relationship between climate change and the global economy may become so intertwined that a higher-than-expected deterioration in the former precipitates an economic depression worse than the one that happened in the 1930s. Financial markets will be extremely volatile amid the uncertainties caused by the Pandemonium scenario.

Although we have selected these flags for the 2020s, it won't necessarily be clear which scenario is in play by the end of the decade. It might take two or three decades before anyone knows which scenario is closest to reality. Nevertheless, the respective flags should give the leading policy-makers in the world some clue of where planet earth is heading in the 2020s – and give them the opportunity to take corrective action.

The flags for the two South African scenarios – People's Economy and Cautionary Tale – can be dealt with more briefly, because there are essentially five flags in total to watch. If they are turning green, the future is moving towards the positive scenario; if they are turning red, South Africa is moving in the opposite direction. They indicate the future like traffic lights. When green, the message is: Go on doing what you're doing and even ramp up the energy to accelerate progress. When red, the message is: Stop and pause to reflect on what is going wrong and revise your plan of action.

The first flag is whether the president of South Africa converts the council of advisers – which was set up to steer the country through the pandemic and thus includes private-sector CEOs – into a permanent body dedicated to the development of small enterprises throughout the country. This would be the best sign that South Africa is setting out on a different track to create an inclusive economy.

At the same time, it would be made clear that any land expropriation designed to create a fairer distribution of ownership will be done on a pragmatic basis with no loss in national food production. An additional sub-flag to watch is the number of new small and micro enterprises created each year, along with the general unemployment rate. If the former is increasing and the latter is dropping, South Africa is heading in the right direction.

The second set of flags includes the performance of state-owned enterprises; the maintenance of public infrastructure and progress on new public projects; and the quality of all key institutions in the education and health sectors. These issues were prioritised in China's extraordinary ascent from a middling economy in the late 1970s to the second largest economy in the world today, and on the brink of becoming number one. That, and liberating Chinese citizens to create wealth for themselves.

The third flag is the Gini coefficient, which measures the inequality of income and wealth in the country. If it is rising, the flag is turning red, and if it is falling, green. This flag will also offer a clue on the levels of happiness and anger among the general population about the state of the nation.

The fourth flag is the number of local initiatives being undertaken to deliver a ground-up revolution in reshaping South Africa's economy. Have big companies cemented their relationship with small companies by making them a larger part of the supply chain? Are local internet stock exchanges being formed in cities to promote the raising of capital by up-and-coming entrepreneurs? Is there growth in the number of companies specialising in micro-lending finance activities to help cash-strapped entrepreneurs, particularly in rural areas? Is there a successful 'buy local' campaign in place, which will, incidentally, lead to a drop in carbon emissions linked to transport? If all the flags are green, we are moving towards People's Economy.

Finally, the fifth flag to indicate which scenario we are heading to concerns the efficacy of law and order. Are the officials alleged to be corrupt being put on trial and, if found guilty, going to jail? Is crime – particularly violent crime – on the increase or decrease? Whether this flag is green or red will clearly signify which path we are on.

Now is the time for some questions, so that you can begin to watch the flags of your own future. Remember that flags come from the big circle beyond your control, and this circle not only represents the world at large, but includes smaller concentric circles representing your country, the industry in which you work, the neighbourhood that you live in and your social network. Your circle of control will overlap with those circles to varying degrees, but their content can change with or without your consent, depending on the level of influence you have in the interface.

1. If you managed to map out any scenarios depicting the future of your own life, using some rules of the game and key uncertainties, what flags would you choose to indicate the probability of each scenario? Which scenario do you think is most probable at the moment?
2. What current flags would give you a sense of the direction your own family and community are moving in?
3. In what ways might you have to change your mind or adjust your strategies as the flags indicating your future possibilities go up and down?
4. Is there a flag that you regret missing because you would have acted sooner to counter the fallout or capitalise on the opportunities of the scenario indicated by the flag?
5. At the other end of the scale, have you ever recognised a flag in time to take full advantage of the future it signalled or perhaps avert disaster?

Hopefully, these questions will convince you that flags are an essential element in thinking the future. You can get ahead of the rest, or perhaps just save your own life.

Chapter 6

The Complexity of Human Nature

When men are most sure and arrogant, they are commonly most mistaken, giving views to passion without that proper deliberation which alone can secure them from the grossest absurdities.
David Hume

Our next giant, David Hume, was a leading Scottish philosopher during the Age of Enlightenment. In the above quote he captures the essence of this book: poor thinking leads to mistaken beliefs. He also rightly points out that such cognitive failures are often coupled with, and masked by, overconfidence. Nowadays, with instantaneous connectivity weaving our world together, misleading portrayals of reality can spread like wildfire across dry veld.

Sometimes it almost feels as if different groups of people live in alternative universes created by conflicting political beliefs. Completely contradictory descriptions are given of the same fact. Few question their own descriptions, because their ideological stance trumps their critical faculty. What is being said is *really* true as far as they're concerned and, if you dispute it, you qualify as the enemy. The Hegelian dialectic – the tension between thesis and antithesis leading to a higher level of truth called synthesis – is, for all intents and purposes, dead in the world of social media. In this context, echo chambers formed by online algorithms have expropriated the land of truth, with little compensation. We're just left with the temporary joy of likes.

Poor thinking about the future is subject to the same frailties. Predictions are often framed along emotional lines or carved according to the shape of one's faith in a specific political or economic cult. Most familiar to us are single-future forecasts by so-called experts, which turn out to be speculative punditry dressed up as deep analysis. These predictions are then further skewed by the medium in which they're presented – narrowed for a bold newspaper headline, exaggerated in a tweet, or spun into a snappy snippet for panel-based television news shows.

Conversely, in looking back at some of history's greatest thinkers, we've endeavoured to bring to light robust arguments for a more effective way of thinking the future. We should do so with an appropriate awareness of our limitations, with a mind open to accepting compelling evidence, and with sufficient imagination not only to challenge orthodox assumptions, but also to develop plausible scenarios instead of a single projection of the future. A deep understanding of the roots underpinning good thinking is essential for this endeavour.

Few people have shaken the tree of knowledge that springs from those roots more rigorously than David Hume. Immanuel Kant – an eighteenth-century German philosopher responsible for some of philosophy's most probing thoughts – credits Hume for wakening him from his 'dogmatic slumber', presumably while nesting up in the clouds among the top branches of the tree. One of Hume's most challenging arguments not only threatened to loosen the leaves of the tree, but to shake the very trunk from which various beliefs about the world branched off. It questioned our previously steadfast assumptions of cause and effect. Applying this to the future leads to some scary conclusions, but also to some powerful lessons.

Playing Games with the Future

Imagine you're playing a game of pool. You're standing next to the table, perhaps sipping a beer, watching as your opponent pulls back her cue and firmly strikes the white ball. It races across the green baize towards a lonely red ball in the middle of the table. White strikes red. What happens next? Presumably the energy from the white cue ball will be transferred to the red ball, causing the red ball to roll on with its own motion. Hopefully, for your sake, not in the direction your opponent intended it to go. Even if you can't describe the physics of the situation, you know enough about life on earth to predict what effect the white ball will cause when it strikes the red.

In *A Treatise of Human Nature*, however, Hume claims that your assumption about what happens next is not actually supported by reason, but rather is a matter of *custom*. We're *habituated* into trusting this instance of cause and effect based on the number of times we have experienced similar instances in the past. Preposterous as it may sound, his argument can be understood via his distinction between different ways of coming to understand things in the first place.

Reasoning, according to Hume, comprises either relations of ideas or matters of fact. This is known as Hume's fork. For example, in mathematics, we don't need to go out into the world, measuring equipment in hand, and experience things in order to deduce various conclusions such as $1 + 1 = 2$ or the radius of a circle is half the length of its diameter. These conclusions are derived from the premises on which the whole mathematical system is based – they only have to be consistent with them. Such an approach is called an analytic *a priori* justification – done *prior* to going off and experiencing things. We could think them through while sitting in an armchair.

The alternative is to infer that something is true, having had an experience in the real world that could justify its veracity. Hume saw this as a synthetic *a posteriori* justification, given after enough empirical evidence has been gathered. This we can't do while sitting at home; we need to get out and about. As smart as Isaac Newton was, he needed to observe an apple falling in his garden at home to have a moment of revelation about gravity, or an epiphany, as some call it. Like Newton, for us to understand the law of gravity, as well as other physical laws of nature, we have to experience them first. We only discover the laws by inferring them from *matters of fact*.

Back to the pool table. Imagine the exact same scenario as we painted earlier on, but this time you have zero experience. Not only have you never played pool, but you have never experienced *anything* before. You don't know what friction is and you've never run your finger along a surface. The concept of 'mass' is foreign, as you haven't held anything before. You've never seen a pendulum swing, a car move or watched something fall to the floor.

Now try to answer the same question: What happens when the cue ball hits the red ball? You wouldn't know. Will the cue ball just stop? Maybe it will bounce back in the direction it came. Perhaps the red ball will shoot up into the air. We can only understand what would happen next by using our familiarity with physical laws that we've experienced in the past.

Our everyday lives are similar. To understand what may happen in the future, we rely on past experience and knowledge. The *only* way we can surmise plausible scenarios for the future is to build them off the knowledge base generated through our experience – with an awareness of the limitations of that knowledge. Hume's tree-shaking impasse, however, rattled the apparent validity of relying on past experience at all.

Hume asserted that all reasoning concerning matters of fact seems to be founded on the principle of cause and effect. But he argues that the assumption of cause and effect between two events is not *necessarily* true. What actually happens is that we draw conclusions about our experience using an implicit principle that the future will be like the past. And this is a principle for which there is no proof. Consider the following Socratic dialogue between yourself and Hume:

You: The sun has just set, David. I'll finish my work when it rises again tomorrow.

Hume: How do you know the sun will rise?

You: What do you mean? It always rises. It's risen every morning of my life, without fail.

Hume: Okay, but why should we rely on past experience?

You: Well, because relying on past experience has always worked.

Hume: So, are you saying that past experience leads you to think that past experience is reliable?

You: … I am.

Hume: You're not providing any justification. You're simply affirming the conclusion you are trying to justify. In other words, your argument is circular.

While we don't know for certain whether the sun will rise tomorrow, we're confident it will. For Hume, we're *habituated* to believing its reliability – it's nothing else but a matter of *custom*. On account of this quite radical doubt, Hume is referred to as a Sceptic. He delved into the foundation of our justifications and showed that it was full of cracks. If this is making you worry about your grasp on reality, don't. Hume didn't think this level of doubt should feature in our everyday lives and admitted that 'none but a fool or madman will ever pretend to dispute the authority of experience, or to reject that great guide of human life'.

His conclusions may be unnerving, but we need to put them in perspective. Much of our knowledge of the world can still be considered rock solid. Indeed, experimental science is founded on the reliability of inference from experience. Nevertheless, Hume's scepticism helps us to be fully aware of how we come to that knowledge, and its inherent limitations.

Scientists are acutely aware of these limitations. They evaluate their theories by repeating experiments over and over again. They also know from Karl Popper's concept of falsifiability that any statement they make must be capable of being disproved for it to be useful. In fact, the quality of scientific research is measured not only by studies that confirm a hypothesis, but by the efforts made to *disprove* it.

Moreover, genuine scientists qualify their approaches with an understanding that their conclusions can always be revised. Einstein's General Theory of Relativity was an advance on Newton's gravitational laws and, since then, our understanding of quantum mechanics has upended the stability of deterministic laws altogether.

Ironically, although Einstein's legacy is defined by his revolutionary ideas, he became somewhat stuck in the thinking that made him famous and initially dismissed quantum mechanics. He could, at least, acknowledge the irony: 'To punish me for my contempt for authority,' he said, 'fate made me an authority myself.' His is a good cautionary tale for reminding us that science is never static – it is always evolving. Hubris is the enemy, and searching questions are the wheels driving discovery. American Nobel Prize–winning physicist Richard Feynman captured this testing relationship between assertion and doubt in a paper titled 'The Uncertainty of Science'. He said:

When the scientist tells you he does not know the answer, he is an ignorant man. When he tells you he has a hunch about how it is going to work, he is uncertain about it. When he is pretty sure of how it is going to work, and he tells you, 'This is the way it's going to work, I'll bet,' he still is in some doubt. And it is of paramount importance, in order to make progress, that we recognize this ignorance and this doubt. Because we have the doubt, we then propose looking in new directions for new ideas.

Feynman summed up his views by describing scientific knowledge as a body of statements, some of which are most unsure, some nearly sure, but none are absolutely certain.

For thinking the future, it is similarly crucial to understand our limits, including the fact that we rely on experience. In one sense, it's all we *can* rely on. We have nothing else to go on, and we are customarily disposed to trust its reliability. However, in another sense, we must be aware of its limitations. Knowing that our inferences from experience are essentially a matter of habit, rather than being fully justified through reason, shines a light on the potential for us to get things wrong. It was customary in days of yore to think that the earth was flat, and that the sun revolved around the earth instead of the other way around. Just as scientists structure their thinking to limit the margin of error, so, too, must futurists employ rules to think the future more effectively and differentiate what is reasonable from what is dogma born out of custom.

We have sought to expound possible rules for thinking the future more effectively in this book. Thinking like a fox means entertaining a range of perspectives and trying to understand things for what they are without trying to include them in, or exclude them from, any one unitary inner vision. To create more robust estimates of what the future may bring, we must continually question our underlying assumptions so that we don't get carried away with speculation based on inherently flawed foundations.

Paying due attention to the uncertainty of the future means thinking in terms of multiple possible futures – scenarios – rather than just relying on a single projection. And, just like scientists, futurists should always be willing to revise their analysis when rising or falling flags indicate a change in the content or probability of a scenario.

All of these points have been about *thinking* the future. But, as we know, a large part of being human means managing that other side to us: our emotions. In tackling this subject, David Hume throws a rope around our now badly shaken tree of knowledge and threatens to rip it out of the ground.

Reason is the Slave of Passion

David Hume's thoughts on the role of reason and the passions are some-times taken out of context. You are likely to have heard his quote 'Reason is the slave of passion'. It alerts us as to how we, as emotional beings, are sometimes whipped up into a state driven more by how we feel than by rational thought. Stoics would advise us to be aware of this possibility, and to reduce the likelihood of getting carried away by emotion by using some simple mental techniques, including the delineation of what is within and outside of our control.

However, that quote is the short version of what Hume actually wrote, and the fuller version offers a more compelling picture for those aspiring to good futures thinking. Hume goes one step further than we might other-wise think in defining reason's ranking in relation to the passions. He said: 'Reason is and ought only to be the slave of the passions and can never pretend to any other office than to serve and obey them.'

So, he acknowledges that our emotions hold more power over us than our judgement, but what's surprising is that he thinks it *ought* to be this way. Why would such a figure, famed for his ability to reason, agree that reason should be subservient to our passions? The answer is that although reason makes sense, it is motivationally inert.

To understand this, consider robots. As technology advances, the capa-city for machines to do complex calculations and computations increases exponentially. But one of the summits that machines have yet to reach, and which those who live in fear of them hope they never will, is where they genuinely feel emotions. Until that point comes along, if it ever does, there is an element of human touch that needs to be involved in configuring machines to carry out certain tasks. We are the reason they do what they do. We are the motivation behind the tasks they carry out.

The word 'robot' comes from the Czech word *robota*, meaning 'forced labour'. It was first coined in Karel Čapek's 1920 play titled *R.U.R.*, which stands for Rossumovi Univerzální Roboti (Rossum's Universal Robots). A robot, as such, is a mechanical representation of 'a slave to the passions'. Indeed, they are slaves to *our* passions. Furthermore, Hume would say robots will always be our slaves, however brilliant they become at computation.

Without passions and emotions, they lack all motivation. They don't have the desire to get up in the morning.

Our ability to reason likewise lacks impetus. The left side of our brain, associated as it is with logic and rationality, is the organic equivalent of the inner workings of a highly advanced robot. It cannot be the origin of our motivations. Through reasoning, for example, we can construct complex utilitarian systems designed to generate maximum happiness for the maximum number of people, but we wouldn't bother doing that at all if we didn't long for happiness in the first place – we can't reason why we ought to want it. Our desire to improve the welfare of sentient beings comes from what British philosopher Julian Baggini calls a kind of 'moral sympathy'. That's the stuff of our passions, which emanates from the right side of the brain, linked to creativity and emotion.

Let's look at two examples to clarify this point: one involves paper clips and the other an incident in the heat of battle. In the first instance, Swedish philosopher Nick Bostrom described a thought experiment where a supercomputer enabled with artificial intelligence (AI) is given the task of efficiently creating paper clips.

As the computer develops more sophisticated ways to do this, it co-opts new techniques to produce millions of paper clips by leveraging various resources. Eventually, the task set by humans becomes a threat to them. Without pre-defined ethical parameters to value human life, the AI supercomputer starts to turn everything in the universe, including humans, either into paper clips or machine parts to manufacture paper clips.

In this example, artificial intelligence has all the reason required to fulfil a set task. However, it lacks the emotional capacity to see the moral limits of its actions. Turning the whole world into a giant paper-clip factory violates all kinds of ethical guidelines and fulfils no need or desire. But that doesn't matter to a computer, because it has no feelings. It has purpose devoid of passion.

This may sound far-fetched to you, so let's go to the positive end of the spectrum and tell a true story of humanity at its compassionate best. On 20 December 1943, an American B-17 Flying Fortress called *Ye Olde Pub* embarked on a mission to bomb an aircraft production facility in Bremen, Germany, but was hit by anti-aircraft fire before it could release its bombs.

While its pilot, Charlie Brown, struggled to get the aircraft away, it suffered a second attack, which killed one of the ten crew and wounded most of the others.

Ace pilot Franz Stigler spotted the crippled US bomber while refuelling and rearming his German Messerschmitt Bf 109 G-6 on a nearby airfield. He took off and quickly caught up with the B-17. Stigler had twenty-seven victories to his name at this point, and *Ye Olde Pub* would make for an easy twenty-eight. As he lined up the enemy in his sights, though, he noticed that the crew were seriously injured, and he remembered the words of a commanding officer while fighting in North Africa: 'If I ever see you shooting at a man in a parachute, I will shoot you myself.'

Stigler decided that the enemy was in the equivalent of a parachute and he couldn't shoot them down. He escorted them out of German airspace and over the North Sea, risking a court-martial for sparing the enemy. He then saluted them and swung back home. Charlie Brown landed the B-17 at a British airbase and, except for one crew member who was killed over Bremen, all survived. A miraculous escape, you might say, although Hume would prefer you to avoid the word 'miraculous', as you will soon learn.

Now comes the part of the story where you may need a handkerchief. In 1986, after relating the incident at a combat-pilot reunion event in Alabama, Brown decided to try to locate the German pilot. After four years of searching, he wrote a letter to a combat-pilot-association newsletter. Stigler, who was by now living in Canada, saw it and wrote back, saying he was the one and confirming the details of what took place. They reconnected and remained close friends until 2008, when they both died within months of each other.

To those of us with even a semblance of humanity, this is an inspiring tale of merciful forbearance. That's because we're not purely rational beings. A large part of our make-up is emotional. And although convention dictates that we should never disobey a command given from above, particularly in war, there's a line we cannot morally cross – no matter what the rationale is behind it. Purely logical robots would follow orders without internal debate. And this is analogous to what Hume thinks may be the result of a human world stripped of our passions. It would be inferior to the one we live in.

Our passions belong to a category of perception that Hume likes to call impressions, which are more lively and vivid than the category of ideas, which arise from reflection. Impressions shape the broad direction for our actions and provide the motivation needed to carry them out. Intelligence agencies, which are designed to mitigate the public's fear of security threats, will think the future in a way that diminishes those threats over time.

Equity and currency traders think the future to serve profit-driven motives and to take advantage of being first movers in the market. Parents think the future when deciding where to live or send their children to school. Thinking the future has no value as an end in itself. Rather, it is a way for us to shed light on the circumstances that can affect the specific ends we *do* value. These ends, Hume believes, are largely framed by our passions.

Thus, we need to recognise that we get emotional about the future because of the value it holds for us. The future contains our dreams, hopes and desires. It dominates our fears and suspicions, and it causes excitement. Hume would not only say that we cannot avoid this fact, but that we *shouldn't* avoid it.

Hume's points about human nature bear out what we said in the previous chapter about flags and how they help us temper our emotions. We are prone to plotting scenarios that encompass our desires. At the same time, we avoid contemplating scenarios that highlight any inconvenient truth that may dash those desires. In other words, poor futures thinkers tend to get carried away by their emotions, meaning their reason becomes clouded and their judgment compromised.

To avoid this, we must be as objective as possible in selecting a range of scenarios that illuminate the good, the bad and the ugly in life. Along with positive flags, we must force ourselves to look at negative flags that suggest we could be moving into territory that does not appeal to our passions. Emotion may still be the boss, but reason needs to be delegated enough authority to make the scenarios credible and consistent.

Understanding this relationship between our passions and our reason is also crucial in accounting for the actions of others. Even Isaac Newton got emotional when he lost his savings in the South Sea Bubble of 1720, moaning that he could 'calculate the motions of heavenly bodies, but not the madness of people'. Most scenario work is about what may happen as a result of human interaction, and this is where the unpredictability lies.

Whether it is the future relationship between nations shaping the global economy, between the various prominent stakeholders making up society or between companies that make up an industry, people and their passions are behind it all. If the scenarios we paint rely too heavily on logic and evidence, we may well miss out on what actually happens in our human, emotional world.

Human history does not repeat itself like a chemical reaction. There is an irreducible zone of uncertainty provided by the human factor. Even in our pool example, where the deterministic laws of physics decide where the white and red balls will end up, it is free will that gets the white ball rolling in the first place. To this extent, the human factor plays a central role in the formulation of scenarios.

However, for a full account of the range of human behaviour and the forces driving it, we need to go beyond reason and the passions. We also need to delve into the concept of faith.

You Gotta Have Faith – Within Reason

The Infidel and the Professor by Dennis Rasmussen tells a funny story of when legendary economist Adam Smith first came across the ideas of David Hume. At the time, Smith was a young buck at Balliol College, Oxford. Hume was more established as an intellectual but was considered something of an outsider. He was agnostic, probably atheist, at a time when such beliefs – or lack thereof – were equivalent to standing in a crowded room holding a sign saying, 'Shun me.'

Smith must have said or done something to arouse the suspicions of his orthodox Balliol dons, because they stormed into his room one day and were aghast to find Smith poring over one of Hume's books. The gown-clad inquisitors snatched the heretical book and gave Smith what can only be termed a Balliol admonishment. Despite the cost he incurred through his curiosity, Smith felt inspired by Hume. They became great friends, and Smith credits Hume for being a hugely influential figure in his own work and life.

Beyond being a humorous anecdote, the story clearly accentuates a distinction between different approaches to belief. Instead of encouraging Smith to read widely, with curiosity and balance, the Balliol dons didn't want him to rock the boat on an issue like belief in God. Hume's work wasn't seen by these clever men as an opportunity to develop a rounded understanding in the learner; it was seen as a threat to Smith's soul.

This is why Hume was particularly suspicious of religion. He was distrustful of attempts to sweep critical thinking under the carpet. If something was to be worthy of belief, it required appropriate justification. Engaging with a diverse array of claims and counterclaims was a healthy way to arrive at truth. Without critically engaging with each element inherent in a certain belief, how could we test its veracity?

One of the religious elements Hume took aim at was the concept of miracles. His work, *On Miracles*, remains a seminal exploration of the idea to this day. By definition, he said, a miracle is 'a violation of the laws of nature'. That time your friend said she once bent a spoon with her mind violates our understanding of physics. Hume believed we should assess each claim on its merits, and miraculous claims needed extraordinary evidence. He didn't think they should be dismissed out of hand, but he demanded the proof.

If none could be given, he acknowledged that you could still believe in a miracle, but it required *faith*. Most religions are replete with miraculous events. In the absence of reason facilitating belief in such events, Hume says faith steps in as a substitute. It's a lovely idea – to trust in something when reason doesn't take us far enough to believe in it. Nevertheless, Hume asks us to recognise faith for what it really is. It's not simply the absence of reason and a convenient plug for what's missing in the gap. Faith actively goes *against* reason; it requires us to abandon our talent for assessing the consistency of everyday events against past experience. Hume said:

> And whoever is moved by faith to assent to it, is conscious of a continued miracle in his own person, which subverts all the principles of his understanding, and gives him a determination to believe what is most contrary to custom and experience. You can believe in miracles as a matter of faith, not reason.

But, in typical fashion, Hume balanced the harshness of his sceptical position with an empathetic understanding of humanity. He recognised that we are naturally predisposed to want to assent to certain beliefs, specifically ones that excite feelings of surprise and wonder, as these are 'agreeable emotions'. Happiness is, after all, about having agreeable emotions and instilling those emotions in others. How often do we proclaim faith in someone else's ability to do something to give that person a jolt of motivation? He or she may have to earn more of our trust along the way, but words of encouragement may become their own self-fulfilling prophecy.

Mahalia Jackson, a famous American gospel singer in the last century, described faith and prayer as vitamins for the soul. Alexis de Tocqueville, a noted French commentator on American politics in the nineteenth century, said that 'Liberty cannot be established without morality, nor morality without faith.'

Just as Hume tempered his refusal to accept faith as a source of empirical wisdom by admitting that it led to agreeable emotions, he moderated his enthusiasm for faith as an emotional stimulant by expressing these words:

> Admiration and surprise have the same effect as the other passions; and accordingly we may observe, that among the vulgar, quacks and projectors meet with a more easy faith upon account of their magnificent pretensions, than if they kept themselves within the bounds of moderation.

Thinking the future is subject to the same vulnerabilities. We can get distracted by the sparkle of events that could revolutionise our lives. Alternatively, we can get spooked by scenarios of Armageddon that may warp our perception of what is plausible and what is not. A competent futurist may well imagine such world-changing events before they happen, but no assertion about the future should be based on faith alone – or driven by the expectation that such an assertion will get more attention.

What we learn from Hume's discussion on miracles is that we need to subject every rule of the game, every key uncertainty, every scenario and every flag to the same probing analysis we use to understand our trusted everyday experiences. If we are proved correct and the future unfolds in a way that is captured by the analyses, it should never be seen as a stroke of good fortune, but as the product of hard work and unrelenting research with no special powers of prophecy involved.

Equally, we must never fall into the trap of believing that certain events will come about because we want them to (or fear that they will) – a claim often spouted by motivational gurus and speakers. Rather, we must reflect on *how* they might materialise, and judge their likelihood with an entirely open mind.

Despite our reservations about faith playing any role in thinking the future, we want to acknowledge that faith is an incredibly important and enriching aspect of our spirituality. Billions of people follow one religion or another. Faith can divide us, but it can also spur people to do things that are beyond the call of duty. It can make them more aware of the ethical compass we cover later in the book.

Finally, futures thinking must be followed by doing something about it, and nothing gets things done like faith in yourself. Foxes have faith in their agility to adapt to whatever life throws at them, yet they would also accept that, like the future, human nature is complex and warrants the nuanced approach that Hume took to it.

There's a story that Adam Smith told about Hume after his death in 1776. He recalled Hume saying to him that he would talk to the ferryman, whose job it was to carry departing souls across the river Styx from this world to Hades, and ask to be given a few more years of life to see 'the downfall of some of the prevailing systems of superstition'. The ferryman responded: 'You loitering rogue, that will not happen these many hundred years. Get into the boat this instant.'

Well, it's been two and a half centuries since Hume died and many superstitions remain alive. He is still a very relevant giant, even if he got the prediction about the duration of some superstitions wrong. He was, after all, being driven by a desire to live a little longer.

Now for the questions:

1. Do you agree with Hume that reason is the slave of passion, or would you say that the human species is more rational in general than he surmises?

2. How do you handle your own emotions when trying to think about some tricky problem? Do you try to think more logically, or do you believe that your feelings, or your 'gut', can guide you?
3. As we enter the third decade of the twenty-first century, which passions do you see coming to the fore and which are declining?
4. Take a set of scenarios you've imagined and reflect on them using the lessons in this chapter. Has your sense of probability been distorted by futures you deeply fear or desire? Did you perhaps pick a flag because you're personally obsessed with it? Have you hung your hopes on a change in someone's behaviour because you will like that person better for it?
5. How should the various religions adapt in order to cope with the increasingly secular world we live in? What future scenarios do you see for the role of religion in the world?

A pertinent way to end this chapter is with a quote from the Netflix series *The Queen's Gambit*, about an orphaned chess prodigy called Beth Harmon. Her chess-playing friend Harry Beltik offers her this advice: 'Anger is a spice. A pinch wakes you up, too much dulls your senses.' Be a clever slave to your passions if you want to win the game.

Chapter 7

Adaptation and Innovation

Ignorance more frequently begets confidence than does knowledge.
Charles Darwin

The quote above is yet another warning that you should not trust over-confident experts, and to be wary lest you become overconfident yourself. Inversely, it's also a statement about how true knowledge brings with it the insight that you do not know everything. That has been our refrain throughout this book: acknowledging our limitations plays a critical role in thinking the future.

Charles Darwin, our next intellectual giant, made that comment on ignorance in *The Descent of Man*, published in 1871, but we want to concentrate on his more influential book, published three years earlier in 1868. *On the Origin of Species* revolutionised our understanding of evolutionary biology and how we originated as a species. In it, Darwin put forward the idea that adaptability is fundamental to survival.

The theme of adaptation has since emerged in many forms of literature. 'Adapt or perish, now as ever, is nature's inexorable imperative,' said H.G. Wells, a noted futurist and the author of *The Time Machine*. The novel popularised the concept of time travel – which, in a way, is the subject of this book. Wells foresaw the introduction of aircraft, tanks and space travel. No wonder he is often seen as the father of science fiction.

This is not to say that you should disregard ambition to change the world in favour of merely adapting to it. As we demonstrated in Chapter 3, your actions could influence the larger environment and change its configuration forever. Playwright George Bernard Shaw said: 'The reasonable man adapts himself to the world; the unreasonable one persists in trying to adapt the world to himself. Therefore, all progress depends on the unreasonable man.' We hope this chapter will help you find a balance between changing the world and changing yourself when approaching the future.

In 1882, the year of his death, Darwin was considered to be one of the greatest scientists of his age and a giant of history. Even the very church his theories challenged accorded him a full state funeral and a distinguished place of burial in Westminster Abbey.

(Incidentally, in his nineties, George Bernard Shaw mounted a campaign to have the ashes of Clem's great-great-aunt, Beatrice Webb, and her husband Sidney, reinterred in Westminster Abbey from their home in Liphook, Hampshire. They were both prominent members of a socialist think tank called the Fabian Society, and were among the founders of the London School of Economics. The campaign succeeded and they are side by side in the abbey.)

HMS *Beagle* and the Legacy of its Supernumerary Naturalist

Born into a family of free thinkers, Darwin developed a taste for natural history and collecting specimens as a young lad. He learnt about taxidermy at the age of sixteen and later assisted in an investigation of marine invertebrates and the classification of plants at the Edinburgh University museum. He left the university without obtaining the degree in medicine for which he was studying, and went on to Cambridge University, where he was awarded a Bachelor of Arts.

During his time there, his cousin introduced him to entomology, and he started collecting beetles. A turning point was reading John Herschel's *Preliminary Discourse on the Study of Natural Philosophy*, which argued that the laws of nature should be worked out through inductive reasoning based on observation. This is much like Aristotle's worldview in contrast to his tutor Plato's, and it matches our emphasis on being objective about judging the evidence gathered from the circle beyond your control.

Just after leaving university in the middle of 1831, Darwin received an invitation to join the HMS *Beagle* as a naturalist and collector on a two-year voyage to explore and chart the coastline of South America. The voyage lasted five years instead of the intended two, encompassing the Galapagos Islands in the Pacific Ocean, and a visit to Cape Town at the southern tip of Africa.

Darwin collected numerous specimens of wildlife and fossils and kept a meticulous journal of all his experiences. After his return to England in 1836, he gradually developed his theory of natural selection, where small, random mutations allowed certain animals to interact more successfully with their environment, survive longer and reproduce at a greater rate, thereby passing those useful mutations on to their offspring. Meanwhile, animals that didn't inherit those changes to help them fit into their environment were more likely to die, and in many cases became extinct. This struggle for existence explains how such a large variety of species could have evolved over time from common ancestors.

Darwin's conclusions are the cornerstone of modern biology, but his principle about adaptation to suit the environment is equally crucial in the world of human affairs and in our foxy approach to futures thinking. You have to develop the eyes and ears of a fox to check out any changes to your surroundings, and you have to use the swiftness of a fox to revise your actions accordingly.

However, there is one crucial distinction to be made. In the theory of evolution, it is a random sequence of genes that leads to change. It's not something you can control (yet). In daily life, though, we can decide whether or not to change as we please. Good luck, bad luck and the myriad things beyond our control still affect our fate, but adapting to the future according to Darwinian principles can reduce the odds of the future being our worst-case scenario.

The phrase 'survival of the fittest' is also associated with Darwin, but was actually coined by Herbert Spencer, a prominent Victorian anthropologist. Spencer had used it to describe the concept of natural selection in his commentary on *Origin of Species*, and Darwin adopted the phrase in later writings. He gave Spencer full credit, although he was slightly worried about the lack of compassion that the phrase implied.

Frequently (mis)interpreted to suit an array of fields and agendas, 'survival of the fittest' has since been used to justify capitalism on the one hand, with competition in an open market being the best way to improve the quality of life; and socialism on the other hand, because cooperation among people often produces a better overall result than individuals competing against each other. In terms of thinking the future, we use the phrase to mean survival of those who best adapt to the changes taking place in the environment around them. Thus, it becomes an acceptable philosophy for a fox to pursue.

The Frailty of Success

As mentioned in Chapter 4, the larger and more successful a company is, the more unwilling it is to change. Success breeds obstinacy to new ideas, and even Einstein wasn't immune to this problem. It strengthens the belief that the formula that propelled the company to the top will continue to reproduce stunning results. The gold medal will go on being pinned to the CEO's tracksuit, year in, year out.

A brief glance at corporate history reveals the exact opposite to be true: sheer size can prevent a company from fulfilling the Darwinian imperative of keeping up with the times and instead turn it into a member of an endangered species. It doesn't usually happen overnight, and there is a brief period of living in a fool's paradise. However, there's a reason why we refer to people and institutions that can't, or won't, evolve as 'dinosaurs': they eventually disappear. For a business sliding into the same category, there are only two options: transformation or liquidation. It's Scylla or Charybdis; take your pick. Many famous department-store chains around the world have suffered this fate.

Having built his own corporate colossus, Amazon CEO Jeff Bezos insists that to survive, it should always be Day 1 in the company. Day 2, he says, 'is stasis followed by irrelevance, followed by excruciating painful decline, followed by death'. Accordingly, he inserts his original letter to shareholders into every Amazon annual report to remind people that nothing about a business can be taken for granted – no matter how much it has grown.

Successful nations can show even more resistance to change than companies. The rise and fall of the Roman, Ottoman and British empires testify to the temporary nature of vast power. Now America's supremacy is being threatened by the Chinese. It would seem that national pride comes before a national fall. Or, as the ancient Greeks stoically maintained, 'hubris begets nemesis'.

Hernando de Soto, a savvy Peruvian economist, put it just as succinctly as the Greeks: 'The past is many nations' present.' He has advocated for years that small entrepreneurs in the informal sector should be elevated to the formal sector by giving them legal title over their property, so that it is easier for them to obtain credit, sell a business or expand it. Otherwise, as 'extralegals' in the shadows of society, they create their own rules to protect their assets and trade profitably, entering the capitalist underworld that goes unrecorded and untaxed. In light of the loss of so many small enterprises due to the Covid-19 lockdowns, one worries that not enough nations will heed De Soto's advice.

The ultimate irony of Darwin's brilliant work concerns the climate-change emergency. As David Attenborough, the world-famous broadcaster and natural historian, has surmised: 'It's coming home to roost over the next 50 years or so. It's not just climate change; it's sheer space, places to grow food for this enormous horde. Either we limit our population growth, or the natural world will do it for us, and the natural world is doing it for us right now.' Yet, according to Darwin's definition of natural selection, in which the capacity to reproduce is a definitive component of successful survival, we have been a particularly triumphant species.

Homo sapiens has been around for two hundred thousand years. Before 1820, we numbered fewer than one billion. In the two hundred years since then, advances in medicine have allowed us to multiply by almost eight times, to nearly eight billion individuals today. To feed and clothe ourselves, we have created extraordinary numbers of livestock as well: one billion sheep, one billion cattle and twenty-four billion chickens. Compare that to 400 000 elephants and a rapidly declining global population of rhinos, which dropped from 500 000 at the beginning of the twentieth century to just 27 000 now, according to the WWF.

Hence, it is time to reinterpret the guidance we've taken from Darwin and apply it to the broader issue of how we can change the way we live as a species to preserve the rich diversity of fauna and flora that still exists on this planet. It demands the same attention to detail that Darwin gave to the specimens he collected on his trip. After all, there is no Planet B for us to escape to.

Our global scenarios in Chapter 4 zeroed in on climate change; however, ensuring earth's sustainability covers a wider field than that. We need another age of enlightenment, like the one David Hume lived in, to generate new ideas about the purpose of existence.

So far, the examples given to illustrate the interweaving of the circles of control and no control, and how adaptation plays a key role in defining the relationship between the two, have been long-term ones about our natural environment. But the same principles apply in an emergency, where new challenges pop up in a matter of seconds or minutes, requiring you to adapt your strategy and tactics in a swift response. The ball ricochets between the two circles at lightning speed, and each shot you play can either be your last or keep you in the game. The amazing rescue of a junior football team trapped inside a cave in Thailand perfectly demonstrates the principle of adapting to a demanding situation as it develops.

The Thai Cave Rescue

On 23 June 2018, twelve boys, aged eleven to sixteen, entered Tham Luang cave with their twenty-five-year-old assistant coach after football practice. Shortly thereafter, heavy rains partially flooded the cave and blocked their way out. They were reported missing that night, after their coach followed up on calls from concerned parents and found the group's belongings near the entrance to the cave.

Efforts to locate the group were thwarted by strong currents and poor visibility because of the murky water. No contact was made for more than a week, by which time the rescue operation had attracted huge international interest and assistance. Thankfully, the assistant coach had previously been a Buddhist monk and encouraged the children to meditate during the ordeal. As we mentioned in Chapter 3, instilling a Stoic attitude in people experiencing a tough time helps them get through it.

On 2 July, two British divers found the group alive on an elevated ledge of rock about four kilometres from the cave mouth. Rescue organisers began the work of adapting to the situation at hand and discussed various options for extracting the group. Should they teach them basic diving skills to enable their early rescue? Should they wait until a new entrance was found or drilled? Or should they wait months for the floodwaters to subside at the end of the monsoon season and provide oxygen and food in the interim?

Multiple dangers, in particular the threat of more heavy rain and a drop in oxygen levels, forced rescuers to make the decision to bring out the team and assistant coach sooner rather than later. They would be accompanied throughout the journey by experienced international and local divers. Between 8 and 10 July, all twelve boys and their assistant coach were rescued in stages, and the only tragedy during the incident was the death of a Thai Navy SEAL in the process of delivering air tanks on 5 July.

But here's the thing. Over a billion litres of water had been pumped out of the cave during the rescue, but moments after the operation was complete, a water pipe burst, and the main pump stopped working. Water levels rose rapidly, forcing the remaining divers inside the cave to abandon their equipment and leave in a hurry. The rescue could so easily have gone the other way if it had been delayed.

The scale and complexity of the rescue effort is revealed by the estimated numbers involved: 10 000 people, including 100 divers, 900 police officers, 2 000 soldiers and numerous volunteers. Representatives from governments around the world were present. The fact that such a gigantic team could work in concert and still have the agility of a fox to adjust to each challenge as it arose is a credit to everyone involved.

Of course, hedgehogs would have been equally committed to the goal of rescuing the children as quickly as possible. However, to assess the rules of the game in an emergency, evaluate the key uncertainties, plot a range of scenarios under pressure, and adapt rescue tactics as the flags went up or down, some extremely foxy thinking was required.

In defining futures thinking in Chapter 1, we said that the time frame was entirely flexible and depended on the issue in hand. By juxtaposing the immediacy of the Thai rescue story with the subject of long-term environmental sustainability, and demonstrating that the same process of futures thinking applies to both, we hope we have convinced you of the versatility of this approach.

Juggling Innovation with Adaptation

In the workplace, the ability to adapt is often talked about as a great skill set to have for solving problems by coming up with innovative solutions. In terms of our model for thinking the future, we feel these skills are essential for taking advantage of the overlap between the two circles of control and no control at the centre of Stoic philosophy. You can bridge the two circles if you have the mind to do so. You may not be able to change the rules of the game, but you can sometimes influence the development of key uncertainties, which means you can influence the scenarios that flow out of them.

Adaptation does not mean being a slave to circumstance. It means having an awareness of your limits and how you could expand those limits by occasionally using your inventive streak or working in a bigger team. Adapting in this sense can help you make a footprint in the larger circle beyond your control, whether that circle demarcates your family, the community or – as Greta Thunberg would have it – the world. The bread and butter of inventors and activists who are intent on changing the world is not necessarily the unreasonableness George Bernard Shaw drew attention to in his earlier quote. Rather it is to juggle innovation and adaptation to find just the right blend to pierce any barriers that are blocking progress. Similar to questioning and assertion, innovation and adaptation work more effectively as a tag team.

Before revealing how this tag team operates within the mind of a fox, let's start by revealing the most important choice facing humanity today, other than the one to do with climate change: either we do everything in our power to improve the quality of life of our world's poverty-stricken inhabitants (who still vastly outnumber those leading reasonable lives) or we disappear like the dinosaurs. In short, we either innovate and adapt, or we die.

According to Oxfam, the world's 2 153 billionaires currently have more wealth than 4.6 billion people, or nearly 60 per cent of the world's population. Indeed, the coronavirus pandemic has shown that even in America, Europe and the UK, only a small percentage of the population has enough savings to escape serious economic distress. Most people live on the cash they earn each month, and without government relief packages, community support or charity during the pandemic, they would have gone to the wall. Soup and other food queues stretched for blocks, while many shops, restaurants and bars remained shuttered for a painfully long time. It is noticeable that, apart from medical staff on the front line, the groups most affected by the pandemic, in terms of serious illness and death, were those in lower income brackets who could not take the same precautions to protect themselves as those earning higher incomes.

At the same time, since the financial crash of 2008, the returns on the stock market and property, in which the rich invested their savings, have far outstripped the annual increases in salaries and wages granted over the last thirteen years. Many economists admit that, in real terms after accounting for inflation, the average middle-class family in wealthy countries is worse off today than in 2007.

The counterargument from those who passionately believe in a free-market economy is that inequality is not the issue, because capitalism has raised millions of people out of extreme poverty. Neither socialism nor communism has delivered the same level of material upliftment to the deprived classes.

That might have been true in the last century and the first seven years of this one, but recently, even before the onset of the coronavirus pandemic, things have been getting tougher economically for ordinary people everywhere – whatever system they live under. The only exceptions are China and a few other fast-growing economies in Africa and the Far East. The statistics are particularly bad for women. In 2020, Oxfam highlighted that the monetary value of unpaid care work done globally by girls and women aged fifteen and over is at least $10.8 trillion annually – three times the yearly revenue of the world's tech industry. All in all, any reasonable yardstick indicates that the overall level of human welfare and happiness has not significantly improved in the 2010s, and the opening year of the 2020s was a shocker too.

Moreover, we're not getting along better with one another at a time when unity is a rule of the game for tackling climate change. Quite the reverse: divisions between and within nations have intensified. The future looks worse for today's younger generations than it did for older generations when they were the same age. This is unique to the modern era because, compared to their predecessors, the lives of all generations since the 1700s showed consistent improvement through technological and medical advances.

The twentieth century included two world wars and a pandemic (in 1918), which together killed hundreds of millions of people. We've only just entered the third decade of the twenty-first century: What else does it have in store for us? If you strip out emotion and take an objective glance at what might lie ahead in the circle beyond your control, you'd be dismayed at the range of plausible catastrophic scenarios, even if you were a Stoic. Despite the amazing speed with which multiple Covid-19 vaccines were developed in 2020, many nations have struggled to obtain them and adjust to the environment in which they now find themselves. Wall Street may be flourishing, but Main Street is languishing.

In short, the pandemic has made our already abysmal social inequality even worse. As a fox, how can you adapt to thrive in these harsh times, rather than adapt merely to survive? We will give you some ideas by going through our model, as described in Chapter 4.

A new, post-pandemic rule of the game is that plenty of the digital activities fostered by the pandemic will endure because they are cheaper and just as effective as the physical face-to-face versions. For example, physical conferences will be competing with webinars, so foxy conference organisers will be thinking about how to turn their events into wider networking experiences. Or take working from home: many people will now be doing that permanently or alternating it with visits to the office. Innovative foxes will not merely adjust to the new regimen, but will ask adaptive questions: How can I rearrange my life to make home a more interesting place for me and my family? Is there any other paid occupation I can take on to supplement my income in case my company goes under? Can I save time and money now that I no longer have a daily commute? Similarly, an innovative owner of office buildings might already be considering ways to accommodate new activities and work practices in a post-pandemic society. He won't wait for the shift to force him to change.

A key uncertainty is whether socially bonding experiences like eating out or visiting the pub will ever be quite the same again. An innovative fox will ask: What new social activity can I establish to add to the richness of public life after the pandemic is over?

Post-pandemic scenarios will include quick and slow recoveries of the economy in your home country and the world as a whole. Besides adjusting their spending habits depending on their economic prognosis, innovative South African foxes should be conscious of the Cautionary Tale scenario, as described in Chapter 4, because of the pandemic's disproportionate impact on the lives of poorer citizens. How, they will ask, can we roll up our sleeves and shift the odds back to the People's Economy scenario, both in our community and in South Africa at large?

What we learnt from Darwin is that adaptability is key to the survival of a species. As human beings, though, we want more than mere survival – we want happy, fulfilling lives. Adaptation has to be combined with innovation so that you not only respond to the future, you take full advantage of it. Moreover, innovation allows you to expand that sliver of influence between the circles of control and no control to the point where you can instigate a causal chain of events that leaves a permanent impression on the outside world. Teamwork may be essential in fostering the required level of social change in the outer circle.

Interestingly, leading recruitment agencies advise employers conducting interviews to keep an eye out for candidates who consider all possible scenarios before making a decision. They are more likely to adjust to unplanned circumstances than be shocked and disorientated. We would add that those candidates are more likely to innovate, too. Apart from not being disorientated, people who consider a variety of possibilities are more likely to come up with a bright idea that allows the company to thrive rather than merely survive. Innovative foxes smell opportunity and take that one extra step to succeed.

Now for the questions. Remember that Darwin will be stroking the extremely long beard he grew later in life as he assesses your answers:

1. Life will periodically involve some big change in circumstances. When it comes to change and growth, are you accustomed to looking ahead and regularly experimenting with small adaptations, regardless of the present situation? Or do you rely on life-changing external circumstances to give you the motivation to change? Would you call yourself an innovator by nature or do you like to take the lead from others?

2. The Spanish flu pandemic of 1918 was followed by the Roaring Twenties, where people were more interested in learning how to dance the Charleston than recalling the miseries of the First World War and the flu. What changes can you make to keep joy and exuberance alive in your life and the life of others?

3. We hope this chapter has demonstrated the need for both personal adaptation and progressive change in our communities, societies and nations. As individuals or organisations, however, we can only do so much and need to strike a balance. Where do you put your efforts and resources when it comes to adaptation and innovation? Does this reflect your needs and values?

4. In the Darwinian model, mutations in the individual can benefit the species. How might you change on a personal level in a way that positively impacts those around you and the things they value? Alternatively, are there ways in which you want to stay the same because changing those aspects of your character or behaviour might have negative consequences?

5. Have you ever had to face a serious emergency, like the Thai Cave incident, where you had to make snap decisions about the best strategy or very suddenly change your approach? Were you able to do so?

We hope these questions show you how complex life is, and that you must adapt – as well as innovate – because the future demands it.

Chapter 8

Thinking an Ethical Future

The reason why we are never able to foretell with certainty the outcome and end of any action is simply that action has no end.
Hannah Arendt

In Chapter 4 we sketched two positive scenarios, one for the planet and one for South Africa, to encourage people to imagine a better future and maybe do something about it themselves. The first scenario we called Paradise Regained, where we as humans live in greater harmony with nature. The second we named People's Economy, where South Africans create a more equal and inclusive economy. What we want to do now is add an ethical perspective to futures thinking, because it may be the defining vector in meeting the challenges of both scenarios. It may also be the ultimate yardstick for judging our worth as a species.

Our commitment to the ethical dimension of what we do, and how we do it, is a necessary condition for positive change. And if ethics is to play a key role in the advancement of society, then we must think about the future in multiple time frames and achieve a balance between them. The future stretches before us like a never-ending horizon. We try to pick out shapes and spots, but the further into the future we look, the less we can trust our judgement. Our natural capacity to look ahead may allow us to anticipate what may happen in the next few days, but it's much harder to imagine the next few years, let alone the next few decades. If you really want to exercise your mind, try to figure out what the earth will look like in a million years. Maybe an astrophysicist can help.

Scenario planning, whether it be for the short, medium or long term, can further illuminate our lives when it's done on multiple time frames, and each scenario should ideally take into account the other time frames. Just as we can begin to understand how the distant future may unfold with a better understanding of what the short term has in store, there is more value in preparing for the short term with an understanding of what can happen in the more distant future.

It's easy to compromise an ethical framework for short-term gain, whether it be a quick fling while in a permanent relationship, firing an exemplary employee to meet quarterly cost-cutting targets, or exploiting people's private data to drive up yearly sales. The allure of quick wins can lead us to make decisions that harm us, or others, in the long term. Such action is driven by an inability to see the bigger picture or, worse, a willingness to ignore it. When thinking the future, this is a cardinal sin.

Being aware of the consequences of our decisions within the broader context of how they may be considered over the passage of time will ensure that we not only make smart decisions, but that we also make ones that safeguard our sustainability as individuals, organisations, or as a species. David Hume resolutely asserted that the principles of morality could not be derived purely from reason or experience alone. The verbs 'is' and 'ought', he claimed, belong to separate worlds of their own, and neither can be drawn out of the other.

For example, just because we *can* eat meat doesn't mean we *ought* to eat meat. You don't need meat to live a healthy life. Yet many people operate on the faulty premise that we ought to do what we evolved to do. Regardless of your eating habits, Hume was right to point out that this form of reasoning is invalid on its own. This was called 'Hume's guillotine', because he severed the link we often implicitly make between observations of fact and judgements about values. More simply: the way things are is no indication of the way things should be.

Confucius, the great Chinese philosopher who lived 2 200 years before Hume, said that morality was something that emanated from the individual through self-cultivation; it could not be prescribed in an explicit set of external rules. Moreover, virtues such as generosity could be attributed to a person only if they were habitually practised. In other words, you aren't a generous person simply because you made a big donation to charity that one time. As historian and philosopher Will Durant wrote in *The Story of Philosophy*, 'We are what we repeatedly do.'

The same attribute is shared by vice, the opposite of virtue. It needs to be repeated often for the term to be applied to your identity; and that is a fitting introduction to the subject pursued at length by the first giant of this chapter.

The Banality of Evil

Hannah Arendt was one of the most pertinent political philosophers of the twentieth century, not least because she explored the rise and spread of Nazism, the set of extremist political principles adopted by millions of people across her native German homeland, eventually driving this Jewish philosopher to flee to Paris, and then New York, to escape its reach.

Much of her thinking on the subject was revealed in *Eichmann in Jerusalem: A Report on the Banality of Evil*, a fascinating book that focused on the trial of Adolf Eichmann, one of the major organisers of the Holocaust. Although less of a figurehead for evil than Hitler, Eichmann was nonetheless a critical cog in the Nazi death machinery. In fact, he was the bureaucratic incarnation of 'chief executioner'. Despite his critical role in one of the worst crimes in human history, however, Hannah Arendt underlined how his form of wickedness was different from stereotypical assumptions of what evil looks like.

Eichmann was no brilliant psychopath like Hannibal Lecter, nor did he go murderously insane like Jack Torrance of *The Shining*. Rather, Eichmann was frighteningly normal. He was neither strong in character nor particularly smart, and he wasn't so much a monster as he was an employee working to a plan in a spreadsheet. The evil he embodied was banal.

The world was shocked by the crimes Adolf Eichmann committed and the evidence in court was clear. But what interested Arendt was how justice could possibly capture the nature of his crimes when they'd been committed in such a routine and bureaucratic manner. She came to the conclusion that the root cause, which allowed the death machine to drum on with devastating momentum, was a *failure to think* by the people involved in implementing Hitler's ghastly vision.

American philosopher Judith Butler summed up Arendt's view on Eichmann's crime in a 2011 article for the *Guardian*:

Indeed, that for which she faulted Eichmann was his failure to be critical of positive law, that is, a failure to take distance from the requirements that law and policy imposed upon him; in other words, she faults him for his obedience, his lack of critical distance, or his failure to think.

Eichmann was an effective cog in a death machine *because* he didn't reflect on the inhumanity of his actions. Stuck in a singular mindset, without empathy or a broader understanding of how history would reflect on his actions, Eichmann's narrow perspective precluded any genuine ethical reflection. This didn't, and shouldn't, absolve him, but Arendt wanted to draw attention to its peculiarity, and highlight the threat of belief without critical engagement. To quote Arendt in her most famous work, *The Origins of Totalitarianism*:

> The ideal subject of totalitarian rule is not the convinced Nazi or the convinced Communist, but people for whom the distinction between fact and fiction (that is, the reality of experience) and the distinction between true and false (that is, the standards of thought) no longer exist.

This highlights the crux of decision-making when thinking the future. Firstly, we must not allow political spin or fake news to sucker us into a distorted view of reality defined by prejudice. Secondly, and even more importantly, every decision we make needs to be checked in advance against basic moral principles – whatever the context. Your reason should not be reduced to the unthinking slave of someone else's evil passions. Whistle-blowers around the world have demonstrated this point when they bravely speak out about the morally unacceptable actions of their superiors and the organisations for which they work. To get to grips with the essence of Arendt's argument, it's crucial that we understand her conception of the unpredictability and irreversibility of our actions.

Web of Interactions

Hannah Arendt divides our existence into three fundamental categories: *labour*, *work* and *action*. *Labour* is the stuff we do to stay alive. It is that which is necessary for us to sustain ourselves. This includes things like sleeping, eating and, yes, going to the toilet. It's about servicing our most basic biological needs.

Work goes one step further. To some extent, we shape the world we live in. We work on it and create material means of making our lives better or more convenient. We make cars and buildings, write code for apps, make music for enjoyment and design all manner of goods for consumption. Arendt says that we must judge this work by its ability to maintain a world fit for human use.

Action is about freedom and plurality and is the specific trait that distinguishes us from other animals and objects. Her idea of *freedom* is the ability to begin something new – the capacity to do the unexpected. For example, we consciously build communities. That decision to will something into existence is an expression of our freedom. But we can only do this if there are other people to build a community with. And this is where *plurality* comes in. For action to be meaningful, it must exist within a context of engagement with others.

Our action is what makes us political animals. It forms a web of connections that ties us together, and which creates a life beyond mere survival. Understanding Arendt's conception of action, and its component parts of freedom and plurality, can provide insights for thinking an ethical future. She points to two features of action that have inherently future-related dimensions: *unpredictability* and *irreversibility*.

Our actions are *unpredictable* because they are manifestations of our freedom. Our ability to innovate and alter certain situations means that we can set in motion a chain of events, and because this happens in a web of connection with others, the consequences are potentially boundless. This is what Arendt was referring to in the epigraph of this chapter: 'The reason why we are never able to foretell with certainty the outcome and end of any action is simply that action has no end.' As a result, we are unable to predict the full scope of our actions. We have already touched on this point with the circles inside and outside of our control, and how an action in one can have a radical impact on the other.

Then, there's an added twist: not only are our actions unpredictable, Arendt says they are also *irreversible*. In the work category, we can shape and construct an artifact, but if we are unhappy with it, it's possible to dismantle it and start again. Deeds in the action category, however, take place within a web of interrelated human relationships. Every action sows seeds with the potential to sprout unintended consequences for others. This is ever more pertinent for those in positions of power and influence. Whether it be business leaders, politicians, opinion influencers or noted intellectuals, the weight of fame, money, power, control and social media reach means their actions have the potential to plant seeds like mega-farmers – on a massive scale. The ethical implications can be both exciting and alarming.

So, what can we do about these potentially boundless and irreversible actions? Arendt has the antidotes and, again, they're distinctly future-related. Alongside the unpredictability and irreversibility of our actions are measures we can take to mitigate their consequences. We have the power of *promise* and the power of *forgiveness*. These are medicines to mitigate the negative symptoms of our actions and allow us to function in a positive manner.

Instead of turning our back on actions to avoid their potentially boundless consequences, *promising* allows us to demarcate the scope of our intentions. To promise something is to set the parameters for certain actions. By saying to your child, 'I promise to pick you up from school,' you are setting a single intention and defining the parameters of the action to fulfil it. While you could do all sorts of things at 2:30 p.m. that after-noon, you have set your own bounds by telling your child that you will not do anything else but be outside the school gates.

Promising, therefore, is the balm that reduces the unpredictability of action. It alleviates the problem, although it can't be seen as an absolute cure. We can still break promises, or some uncertainty beyond our control may prevent us from fulfilling them.

That leaves *forgiveness* to take on the difficult task of irreversibility. There's no way to stop our actions being irreversible. A constructive follow-up action may undo the harm that was caused, but that subsequent action will, in and of itself, have consequences of its own. Instead, Arendt thinks forgiveness can liberate us from the burden of irreversibility. In *The Human Condition*, she writes:

Without being forgiven, released from the consequences of what we have done, our capacity to act would, as it were, be confined to one single deed from which we could never recover; we would remain the victims of its consequences forever.

Forgiveness allows us to cooperate on a mutual understanding that releasing others from their actions, and being released from our own, is necessary for our future not to be defined entirely by our past. Nelson Mandela's forgiveness of those who caused irreversible harm during apartheid is a good example of this. Through truth, forgiveness and reconciliation, Mandela was able to ensure that South Africa's new dawn was not characterised by vengeance and violence, but rather by hope for brighter times ahead. Forgiveness of the past liberated Mandela to set a new agenda for the future.

The liberation associated with forgiveness is also powerfully captured in the film *The Mauritanian* (2021). The story is based on the memoir of Mohamedou Ould Slahi, who was falsely accused of being part of the 9/11 terrorist attacks, and subsequently detained and tortured in Guantánamo Bay detention camp for fourteen years, without being charged. Towards the end of the movie, Slahi's character (played by Tahar Rahim) says that in Arabic, the word for 'free' and the word for 'forgiveness' are the same. This supports Arendt's categorisation, in which they are two sides of the same coin.

Tracking the Future

Imagine you're standing on a bridge, overlooking two sets of train tracks, running in parallel. Below you, on one set, lie five people tied to the tracks. A train is approaching and will be unable to stop in time. The five seem destined for a nasty death. At your right hand is a lever that can mechanically switch the approaching train onto the parallel set of tracks. You're about to pull the lever when you notice another person tied down on these alternative tracks. It's a young girl. What do you do?

You may think it's surely better to save five lives instead of just one. But if you pull the lever, you'll be complicit in the death of a young child. If you don't pull it, you may be regarded purely as a spectator in an awful tragedy;

after all, you aren't the one who tied all these people to the tracks. Alternatively, it could be said that choosing inaction – not pulling the lever – still makes you complicit. If you could have done something but didn't, then people may argue that you have blood on your hands regardless of the fact that you did not create this problem.

We can further complicate this moral conundrum. What if the group of five victims were all convicts? Would that alter your decision? On the other hand, what if they were family members of the young child tied to the other tracks? None of these are easy choices. They're tough ethical dilemmas that require a combination of reasoned argument and compassion. There's no happy solution, but by thinking the dilemmas through, we can reflect on, and bring nuance to, our ethical decision-making.

Thought experiments such as these were originally made famous by English philosopher Philippa Foot. She is our second giant for Chapter 8. The above example is a variation of her 'trolley problem', which has been widely taught, tinkered with and deliberated on in philosophy and decision-theory classes. Foot was the granddaughter of former US president Grover Cleveland. She studied politics, philosophy and economics at Somerville College, Oxford, where she also went on to be a lecturer, engaging in ongoing debates with fellow prominent thinker Gertrude Elizabeth Margaret (G.E.M) Anscombe.

Foot used these thought experiments to explore the ethical dimensions of practices such as abortion. By imagining alternative scenarios, she was able to point out the coherency, or incoherency, of the justifications for our actions. By slightly adjusting each scenario – casting the people on the tracks as convicts or relatives, for example – one can discover and test ethical boundaries.

If you are willing to let the convicts die, it suggests that you believe their lives have lesser value than someone who has not been convicted of a crime, and perhaps that you believe your government's justice system is fair. If the five adults on the first track are all related to the child on the other, then the dilemma might cause you to reflect on the interconnectedness of human relationships, and how the ones who live will still suffer because of those who have died.

The world's political establishments experienced a real-life version of

Foot's trolley problem during their decisions to implement stringent lock-downs in response to the Covid-19 pandemic. Scientists and politicians had to balance the need to curb the spread of a highly contagious and largely unknown virus against the significant effects of closing down huge swathes of the economy. Equally, it meant denying citizens the rights that most of us had previously taken for granted, such as freedom of movement and to connect with family and friends in person. The dilemma has since been referred to as walking the tightrope between 'lives and livelihoods'. It certainly highlighted the fact that morality has its own versions of sailing between Scylla and Charybdis.

At this point it's worth revisiting Pierre Wack and the methodology of scenario planning. We've stressed the importance of imagining multiple possible futures, rather than projecting a single future in one forecast. We maintained that such an approach encouraged proactive decision-making in the face of an uncertain, changing environment. What we would now like to suggest is that the process of building scenarios also has significant value in helping us explore and refine the ethical dimension of our decision-making with regards to the future.

Suppose you are at a classy restaurant with your partner, perusing the menu. Your partner spots an exotic dish that he or she would like to try, but you realise that most of its ingredients have been flown in from around the world. As a result, the dish must have a high carbon footprint compared to other items on the menu. Do you opt for a short-term scenario of letting your partner enjoy an exciting meal? After all, the ingredients are already there. Or do you try to persuade your partner to have something else to set an example about considering the quality of life of future generations in any decision?

Running through the scenarios in your head will allow you to assess the consequences of each option and reflect, with reference to your own ethical guideline, as to what's best. Have you ever heard a celebrity chef give advice on what the answer should be?

Thought experiments such as Foot's trolley problem should be a staple exercise for all futures thinkers. Playing out possible scenarios allows us to reflect on the set of available options in an ethical dimension and then map out the moral consequences of the action we choose.

In business, for instance, every human resource manager should paint various scenarios of how the workplace policies they formulate could play out beyond their intended effect. Companies that opted to either retain or retrench their workforces in response to the coronavirus pandemic may have focused on the short term, but the ethical nature of those decisions will be remembered by the remaining staff when discussing the integrity of the human resources department.

More controversially, in some legal and investment banking firms, the average junior trainee works a seventy to ninety-hour week. Foot would suggest that more attention be given to personal life on the other track.

CEOs should think twice about accepting huge increases to their remuneration packages in this day and age of inequality, when a company's Gini coefficient, comparing the ratio of salaries at the top to wages at the bottom, is widely quoted. Sheltering the profits of a business in a tax haven may qualify as tax avoidance rather than tax evasion, but the business may lose its reputation in doing so because legal actions may still be seen as immoral.

In politics, every member of parliament should explore the consequences of voting for a specific Bill by asking if it might do harm as well as good. And parents need to put themselves in the minds of their children when deliberating on whether to move to another region or country.

The push to examine our decisions from all angles within a broader ethical context is part and parcel of being a decent human being. We have to think further into the future than the here-and-now mentality of today's world, because one decision, perceived as evil, can undo all the good accumulated over the years.

In his wonderful book *Breaking Bread with the Dead: A Reader's Guide to a More Tranquil Mind,* Alan Jacobs points us in the direction of a poignant phrase first used by novelist Thomas Pynchon. In his 1973 novel *Gravity's Rainbow,* Pynchon employs a concept he calls 'temporal bandwidth', which is the range of time we look backwards and forwards, and goes on to say:

> The more you dwell in the past and future, the thicker your bandwidth, the more solid your persona. But the narrower your sense of Now, the more tenuous you are.

Jacobs's book explores how we can cultivate our temporal bandwidth to gain tranquillity and go beyond the immediate urgencies of the modern world. His approach, as has been ours, is to learn to do this by expanding our knowledge of, and appreciation for, thinkers of the past. This can yield great insights to our present and our future.

As Hannah Arendt notes, the consequences of our actions are irreversible. We can hope for forgiveness, but there's no guarantee that it will be granted. You have to take personal responsibility for your actions, because you are not just part of a system, but an individual with free will. Sometimes you ought to think carefully about the ethics of what's happening and go against the grain for the sake of a higher moral purpose. Our next giant did precisely that and made one of the most iconic speeches in American history.

I Have a Dream

Martin Luther King Jr. was born in Atlanta, Georgia, in January 1929. He gave his first public address in 1944 at the age of fifteen and rose through the ranks to become the most prominent leader of the American civil rights movement from 1955 until his assassination in 1968. On 28 August 1963, at a protest gathering of more than a quarter of a million people for jobs and freedom, he delivered a seventeen-minute speech from the steps of the Lincoln Memorial in Washington, D.C. The most famous passage departed from the prepared text and included the following words:

> I say to you today, my friends, so even though we face the difficulties of today and tomorrow, I still have a dream. It is a dream deeply rooted in the American dream.
>
> I have a dream that one day this nation will rise up and live out the true meaning of its creed: 'We hold these truths to be self-evident: that all men are created equal.'
>
> I have a dream that my four little children will one day live in a nation where they will not be judged by the colour of their skin but by the content of their character.

If anything shows the need for an ethical dimension to futures thinking, it's this speech. Notice that King did not forecast the imminent arrival of a non-racial society; he said it was a dream. In Chapter 4 we said that scenarios should be like movie scripts, designed to enthral an audience, and King did just that by appealing to America's sense of decency and morality, and reiterating the fact that his dream was already part of the American dream. We have injected the same two qualities into the scenarios Paradise Regained and People's Economy: both have an ethical dimension, and both fit within an existing moral ideal.

In the same way that Karl Popper incorporated a range of predictable and unpredictable phenomena using his spectrum of clouds and clocks, we feel that scenarios should balance credibility with enough visionary input to get people's attention. David Hume was right on the button with his conclusion that reason and emotion – though originating from different sources of the human psyche – were both essential in distinguishing human beings from robots. They are also both essential in motivating us to do good things (and unfortunately bad ones, too).

Sadly, as Black Lives Matter and similar movements demonstrate, there is still a long way to go in achieving King's dream. Some may argue life has become more fractured since then. British historian Dame Cicely Veronica Wedgwood, our fourth giant in this chapter, explains why in her typically articulate way:

> Human life is essentially dramatic; it is born and exists in conflict, con-
> flict between men, conflict between men and circumstances, or conflict
> within the confines of a single human skull.

It's this conflict that has led to a messy history of progress and regression. Acknowledging the conflict is what defines a more sensitive and subtle approach to the evolution of history and the various events that shape its character. Wedgwood embodied a characteristically foxy outlook: 'The whole value of the study of history is for me its delightful undermining of certainty, its cumulative insistence of the differences of point of view.'

One of the traits that made her a brilliant historian – and which should sit well with any great futures thinker – was her cold-eyed clarity regarding the deficiencies in our moral make-up. In the introduction to *The King's War, 1641–1647*, her history of the English Civil War, fought between 1642 and 1651, she says the highest ideals at the time were fought for by men who fell short of those ideals. However, she qualifies this with her judgement, gained from reading volumes of history, that even the best of us do not live consistently on the highest plane of virtue and, in most cases, live far below it.

Ironically, the dilemma of fighting for progressive values in a context that fell well short of those ideals was displayed in Wedgwood's very name. Although she was one of the most perceptive historians of the last century, she published her work under the name C.V. Wedgwood to obscure the fact that she was a woman. She was cognisant of the prejudice of her era that readers did not take women thinkers as seriously as men. You may wonder how much has changed since then. Well, in 1997 – the year of Wedgwood's death at the age of eighty-seven – J.K. Rowling's publishers asked that she, too, use her initials rather than her full name, because boys might not read a fantasy novel written by a woman.

The Ethics of Big Tech

One of the defining issues of our time – and likely to become even more important in the future – is the tension between greater online connectivity and availability of data on the one hand, and the ethical parameters surrounding our rights to retain privacy over that data on the other. Companies such as Facebook and Google are coming under ever-increasing scrutiny because of the extensive data collected through our engagement with their platforms and services.

The upside is that by surrendering our data, we can use sophisticated technologies that connect us to each other and to a world of information for 'free'. However, these technologies enable the monitoring of our behaviour to the extent that they can paint a meticulously personalised picture of who we really are – both in our professional and private life.

But, in line with Wedgwood's perceptive observation, you can't escape the inherent conflict. The extent to which our personal data is collected is the extent to which our privacy is violated. There is a tenet that if a product is free, you *are* the product. In the case of social media, you can use it for free because your attention is being harvested and sold to advertisers. Furthermore, the sites and apps are specifically designed to be psychologically addictive and manipulative, without much regard for the harm they are causing.

This conflict will shape the future of Big Tech – Amazon, Apple, Facebook, Google and Microsoft. While their stock prices soar in line with their growing influence and omnipresence, questions are being asked about the pernicious effects of their near-Orwellian pervasiveness. Remember the lesson from the tales of tragedy in Chapter 3: dormant perils lurk behind every act of triumph with the potential to undermine it. The turbo-charged data-vacuuming techniques that have enabled Big Tech to reach such dominance could be the same mechanisms that bring about their demise. The leaders of these companies will need to show real foresight to think a more ethical future.

If not, then a day of reckoning is coming for Big Tech. If they continue to flout generally accepted ethical norms, they will no longer have a friendly climate in which to operate. That is a rule of the game. The key uncertainty is whether they realise it or not. This leads to two scenarios: they voluntarily change their behaviour, and perhaps their corporate structures as well; or governments start forcing them to break themselves up or rein themselves in by enacting new legislation.

At the same time, focusing on immediate gains to keep shareholders happy may result in their pushing the boundaries of personal privacy to the point that people feel it is an immoral invasion. A third scenario then opens up: the users become resentful and start a pushback from the bottom up. Already, documentaries like *The Social Dilemma* are suggesting that young people should avoid letting social media consume a large chunk of their daily routine. The sustainability of Big Tech giants is therefore dependent on how the top brass respond to this challenge. All we can do is watch the flags in terms of their actual behaviour to see which of the three scenarios is the most likely to materialise.

In a wider context, 'survival of the sneakiest' is a term used both in biology and in business. In biology, it refers to those animals who sneak in silently after those with loud mating calls have been devoured by predators, and act as substitutes for reproductive purposes. In business, it relates to companies that sneak into markets, fool consumers into submission and remove competitors in unethical ways. All the while, they mask their true intentions with clever public-relations strategies. Don't be fooled by their seductive, sneaky slogans. You need to dig deeper than that.

The Moral Balance

In this chapter, we have plumbed the depths of evil with Arendt's description of Eichmann; we have explored the problem of choosing the lesser of two evils with Foot; we have reached for the sky with King's speech; and we have brought you back to earth with America's lack of progress in achieving King's dream and the dubious ethics of Big Tech. The ambiguity of humanity's attitude to virtue and vice means that dream or nightmare scenarios will occasionally materialise, but more often than not, reality ends up being something in between. This does not make the future less interesting to contemplate. Rather, it makes the future more complex to analyse, because it comes about through a mixture of virtue and vice. The key uncertainty is where the balance lies.

Foxes sense the difference between doing something the right way and doing the right thing – i.e. between acting skilfully and acting ethically. In our complex and uncertain world, great futures thinkers embrace this difference, but also ask how future generations might judge some of the practices that we consider acceptable or turn a blind eye to today. For example, the philosopher Thomas Nagel offered this line of thought in an article for the *New York Review of Books*:

> Whether we should kill animals for food is one of the deepest disagreements of our time; but we should not be surprised if the issue is rendered moot within the next few decades, when cultured meat (also called clean meat, synthetic meat, or in vitro meat) becomes less expensive to produce than meat from slaughtered animals, and equally palatable. When that happens, I suspect that our present practices, being no longer gastronomically necessary, will suddenly become morally unimaginable.

There are many other current practices that may be morally unimaginable in fifty years' time. The fact that we buy products manufactured through exploitative or forced labour practices could be seen as an acceptance of modern slavery. The conversion of tropical forests into agricultural land is destroying the lungs of this earth. And the behaviour of rich countries towards migrants and refugees seeking a better life undermines some of our basic values regarding human life. Scenario planners are there to turn the eyes of the future back onto the present and question the morality of our actions today.

Wedgwood offers a beautiful metaphor, which simultaneously captures the power of nuance and the art of balancing competing thoughts about the fundamental nature of human beings:

> The individual – stupendous and beautiful paradox – is at once infinitesimal dust and the cause of all things ... I prefer this overestimate to the opposite method which treats developments as though they were the massive anonymous waves of an inhuman sea or pulverizes the fallible surviving records of human life into the grey dust of statistics.

We hope that we've provided you with an ethical compass by which you can assess your bearings and guide yourself into the future. Now for the questions. Introspect carefully before giving the answers, as your reputation and legacy may depend on them.

1. Is the way you conduct yourself in relation to your fellow human beings a fitting yardstick by which other people should judge your moral character? What other qualities do you think are relevant in assessing your worth as a human being? Do you incorporate the ethical dimension in scenarios of your own future?
2. We are all a complex mixture of virtues and vices. Have you tried to revise your own particular mixture in a way that improves your self-image?
3. Have you had a situation where your personal values have made it difficult to conform with certain social, professional or legal requirements? How did you use your ethical compass to steer your way through the moral dilemma created?
4. What contemporary customs do you think future generations will be

shocked that we accepted as reasonable? What is it about these customs that make them problematic?

5. Have you ever been faced with a 'trolley problem', as described by Philippa Foot, where either choice has tragic consequences? What moral conundrums did you endure, and did they make you more aware of your underlying ethical values?

Chapter 9

Thinking and Doing

You cannot plough a field by turning it over in your mind.
Unknown

While the main purpose of this book is to help you think the future in a more productive way, it would be remiss of us not to include a chapter on the crucial interplay between thinking and doing. The triumvirate of thinking, talking and making decisions without doing anything about it leads to many unfulfilled promises in the political sphere – and many failed ambitions in people's personal lives. In addition, doing without thinking about the consequences of what you are doing has led to the downfall of many celebrities and other powerful folk. For the average person, it has often meant living a life you did not intend to lead but blundered into via a series of thoughtless decisions.

A combination of thinking and doing is inextricably linked to lasting success in the real world. The two giants we have chosen for this chapter, Nelson Mandela and Steve Jobs, knew perfectly well that you had to combine the two qualities, and in the right order: thinking, then doing. It made Mandela one of the greatest heroes of modern times, while Jobs has made one of the biggest impacts on life in this century so far. He and his colleagues made great leaps in the design and capability of the technology we now use every day to communicate with one another, and which in turn has transformed the way we live and work.

Action, Not Just Words

Before examining their contributions, we would like to remind you of a point regarding the scenario-planning techniques described in Chapter 4. After defining the rules of the game, identifying the key uncertainties and painting the scenarios, thinking the future like a fox then demands that you consider your best options and make decisions that can be effectively implemented. It is beyond the scope of this book to discuss these two steps in detail, but one crucial point must be made: in judging the different options, do your best to compose narratives of how each one may play out, so that when you make a decision, you can compare the actual chain of events occurring in reality against the intended narrative behind your decision. If they differ markedly from each other, perhaps because something from the circle beyond your control interferes with the planned consequences of your decision, you have to consider modifying it or dumping it altogether in favour of one of the other options. In constantly thinking the future, foxes retain the flexibility to change their strategy and tactics when the circumstances warrant it.

At the other end of the spectrum, hedgehogs, once they are committed, seldom change their mind about anything. This is fine if your decision is absolutely right in the first place, or if you have enough control and influence to make a surprising twist suit your chosen direction. However, if the unexpected change in your environment is completely beyond your control and makes your decision invalid, but you persist in implementing it anyway, then the results can be disastrous.

Nevertheless, unless the best decision is to stay put with your arms folded, nothing should deter you from acting as swiftly as possible after weighing up the different scenarios and choosing the best option. In 1987, Clem published *The World and South Africa in the 1990s* and closed it with the following: 'I hope that this book has sown the seeds of action, because in the end it is only action that counts.' Indeed, Neil Armstrong's words, 'That's one small step for man, one giant leap for mankind,' will reverberate forever in people's minds only because he was the first man to walk on the moon in July 1969.

Equally, the bombastic language of Winston Churchill, which stole the hearts of many Britons, would have sunk into obscurity if he had lost the Second World War. As he himself said: 'I never worry about action, but only about inaction.' He also showed that he was foxy in thinking about the short-term future with the observation that 'It is a mistake to look too far ahead. The chain of destiny can only be grasped one link at a time.'

Nonetheless, he demonstrated his capacity to be a long-term futurist too. He was ahead of the rest of the Westminster establishment in seeing the threat Adolf Hitler posed as he rose to power in the 1930s. In an article for the *Evening Standard* newspaper in May 1936, Churchill wrote the following about the way Germany was arming itself:

> All this (money and labour) gone into making the most destructive war weapons and war arrangements that have ever been known. What is it all for? Certainly it is not all for fun. Something quite extraordinary is afoot. All the signals are set for danger. The red lights flash through the gloom. Let peaceful folk beware. It is a time to pay attention and to be well prepared.

Churchill disregarded Neville Chamberlain's foreign policy of appeasement, believing it would never work with a man like Hitler. Instead, he foresaw a scenario of war involving 'blood, toil, tears and sweat'. He was right but, more importantly, he proved an agile enough leader to defeat Hitler. If he were alive today, we would want to ask him how he felt about the possibility of a nuclear war between the US and China. The two nations are so different and appear to be on a collision course on many issues. Churchill, however, might invoke the principle of mutually assured destruction to say the odds of war are low.

In the recent past, New Zealand prime minister Jacinda Ardern showed a marked preference for action over words. After the Christchurch mosque shootings in March 2019, to which we referred in Chapter 5, she visited the first responders as well as the families of the victims. Less than one month after the attack, the New Zealand government passed a law banning most semi-automatic weapons and assault rifles, parts that convert guns into semi-automatic guns, and high-capacity magazines. Ardern also instituted a government buyback of existing firearms. In contrast, the US government has refused to implement any serious gun reforms despite the upward trend in hate-crime shootings.

In March 2020, Ardern announced the widest-ranging and toughest border restrictions of any country in the world as part of New Zealand's response to the Covid-19 pandemic. As an article in the *Washington Post* put it at the time: 'New Zealand isn't just flattening the curve. It's squashing it.' Arden's lockdown strategy was coherent and clear-cut, contrasting sharply with the confusing and complicated measures of her European, British and American counterparts.

The result is that New Zealand almost banished the virus in one month, whereas other countries experienced further waves. No wonder Ardern was re-elected in a landslide victory in the October 2020 general election. She gets things done in a way that clearly moves the country – if not the world – towards a future that people want.

One note of caution before we introduce our giants. In Chapter 2 we gave great attention to the mistakes in intelligence reports that led to the Iraq War in 2003. The reason for doing this was to warn our readers against hasty action based on faulty intelligence, whether it is gathered by you as the decision-maker or by others. Moreover, you must try as hard as possible not to allow emotion to distort your view of reality. Your thinking, therefore, ought to have some element of Socratic dialogue about it to improve the chances of your resulting action – or decision to desist from action – being the correct one in retrospect.

The Foxy Shepherd

Nelson Mandela was a doer with a consistent and transparent purpose: to steer people towards his ideal scenario and away from those he considered dangerous. He articulated his approach as follows: 'Action without vision is only passing time, vision without action is merely daydreaming, but vision with action can change the world.' In the manner of Churchill, he was also a consummate expert at capturing a future that some of his peers did not foresee when he was released from prison in February 1990.

He believed that a new democratic South Africa could be achieved via a peaceful settlement rather than a civil war. Clem had the privilege of seeing him for a one-on-one conversation at his small cottage on the prison grounds a month before his release. Mandela had read Clem's book, *The World and South Africa in the 1990s*, which presented two scenarios for the future of South Africa: the High Road of negotiation and integration versus the Low Road of continued segregation and violence. He wanted to talk about it, and what followed was five hours of intense discussion about the future, with no exchanges at all about the past – other than a bit of reminiscing over lunch.

Mandela started by reciting a Deng Xiaoping quote from the book: 'I don't care if a cat is black or white as long as it catches mice.' He followed that up by declaring: 'I have spent twenty-seven years in prison, and while I have done my best to keep abreast of developments in the world, I want to know from you what works and what doesn't. I have read your global and South African scenarios, but there is nothing like hearing it from the horse's mouth.'

Clem and Mandela talked about China and how President Deng had infused new energy into the economy by creating a model that allowed Chinese citizens to create their own wealth, while the state concentrated on building a modern infrastructure. Mandela asked whether Russia and Cuba were following China in adapting communism to the new reality, and he and Clem agreed that the two countries were somewhat behind. They looked generally at the role of government and private enterprise in a modern economy and what should be the optimum balance, and discussed education and how its quality could be improved to ensure South Africa became a winning nation. Then they moved on to how capital could be mobilised to accelerate economic growth, and how big companies could work in harmony with small companies to broaden everyone's share of the economic pie. In particular, Mandela wanted ideas on how to minimise corruption so that it did not undermine the national work ethic.

All in all, he wanted to hear about the latest trends in the world, should South Africa be invited back into it by becoming a fully fledged democracy. The trends would then constitute a portion of the rules of the game South Africa would have to adhere to in climbing its way back from sanctions into an open global economy. Mandela seemed to feel that a key uncertainty revolved around the comparative strengths and weaknesses of the free enterprise system versus the socialist model. How would this affect his concept of the desirable and undesirable scenarios he had in mind?

For Clem, it was an introduction to Socratic Dialogue: he made assertions and Mandela questioned them with a skill that came from his legal background. Throughout the conversation, Mandela exhibited his enduring passion for racial reconciliation in South Africa, with no hint of bitterness about his own past. This was astonishing in light of the fact that he had suffered such a long incarceration.

The point of this story is to show that thinking and doing came naturally to Mandela. He himself said: 'A leader ... is like a shepherd. He stays behind the flock, letting the most nimble go out ahead, whereupon the others follow, not realizing that all along they are being directed from behind.' This was his way of subtly entering that crucial overlap between the circles of control and no control.

During the arduous negotiations that occurred after his release, he and F.W. de Klerk would always step in when the talks were on the verge of collapse. When he was elected president of South Africa, he ensured that pragmatism was a centrepiece of government policy by appointing Trevor Manuel as minister of finance in 1996. The country's finances were kept in good shape. Against the advice of many colleagues, he supported the Springbok rugby team and famously wore a Springbok rugby jersey when he was photographed handing the World Cup trophy to team captain Francois Pienaar in June 1995.

Mandela served only one term, saying that an octogenarian should not be meddling in political affairs and he wanted to give over to a younger person, but that he would be there for advice if needed. The economy generally did well under his leadership, although the reforms required to turn it from an exclusive to an inclusive economy subsequently faltered. He also did not eliminate corruption, which remains a major thorn in South Africa's side.

One other incident showed his firmness of character and his ability to weigh up scenarios quickly before making a decision. In 2001, he was invited to be the guest speaker for an event at Hilton College, a private boarding school for boys in KwaZulu-Natal. Unfortunately, his plane could not land at the nearest airport on account of bad weather. When this news was relayed to the headmaster, he presumed that the plane would turn back to Pretoria and he asked Clem, who happened to be there as a friend of a parent, to give an impromptu speech in Mandela's place.

Unbeknown to the school, Mandela insisted that the plane be flown on to Durban, from where he would travel to the school by car – a journey of more than an hour. He had obviously played the scenario of the huge disappointment his absence would cause and vowed not to allow this to happen. To everyone's surprise, he arrived at the college in time to make a short speech. He then handed out the academic prizes to the boys and addressed each one of them. That is why Madiba, to call him by his family or clan name, was universally loved by ordinary citizens. He did what he had promised to do by swiftly thinking through the scenarios and options when caught unawares.

At heart, though, he was a humble man, as summed up in this thoughtful quote: 'Do not judge me by my successes, judge me by how many times I fell down and got up again.' Repeatedly trying again after failing is an important quality to possess, as is considering a different approach next time round to make the desired scenario a reality. Mandela showed the flexibility of a fox in choosing his tactics to get things done, but the perseverance of a hedgehog when his ethical sense of right and wrong was on the line.

A Ding in the Universe

We now turn to the second giant, Steve Jobs, who, incidentally, once said that he would trade all his technology for an afternoon with Socrates. But much more germane to the theme of this chapter, he made this comment: 'The doers are the major thinkers. The people that really create the things that change this industry are both the "thinker-doer" in one person.' This is precisely the message of this chapter.

There is one further point to recall. As you will have learnt in Chapter 4, the rules of the game are factors common to all scenarios. These include trends driving the future in a fairly predictable direction, but *any* reliable assertion about the future can be considered a rule if it's relevant to your scenarios. A recently passed piece of legislation, for example, might be relevant for every scenario no matter what else happens. In our method, the rules of the game can also include requirements for success in a venture, if you are confident enough that they would apply in the future. The key uncertainty is whether you comply with them or not.

Accordingly, we want to use Jobs's exceptional but relatively short life to show that there are rules of the game that apply in any scenario where you become a successful entrepreneur. Despite all those giddy texts and sayings urging you to break the rules to get on in life, we feel the exact opposite when it comes to thinking your future in a creative but realistic way – that is, if you want to turn your ideas into a sustainable and profitable enterprise. For us, identifying the rules for winning is a precondition to achieving the desired scenario in whatever field you choose; so, even though the rules we're about to give you are for entrepreneurship, you can reinterpret them for any career or pursuit.

The first entrepreneurial rule is a contextual one: discover who you are, because business success requires you to play to your strengths and make up for your weaknesses by choosing partners or allies who offset them. Jobs had a complicated childhood. His biological father was Syrian and his mother American, and they gave him up for adoption to Paul and Clara Jobs, who lived in California. He always referred to them as his real parents. Paul, who was handy at making things in the garage, got his son to help him. Young Steve also developed an interest in electronics. At school, he was perceived as a socially awkward loner who hated authority, but he forged a close friendship with fellow pupil Steve Wozniak, which changed his life. After leaving school, Jobs did a course on calligraphy and learnt all about the art of producing decorative handwriting or lettering with a pen or brush. He subsequently said: 'It was beautiful, historical, artistically subtle in a way that science can't capture, and I found it fascinating.' He also read Shakespeare and studied Zen Buddhism, spending seven months in India.

Jobs and Wozniak started Apple in 1976 and hit paydirt with the Apple II in 1977. Wozniak designed the computer and Jobs handled the casing. Herein lies the learning of the first rule. Jobs was passionate about how a product looked and felt to the human touch. He used this personal quality to Apple's advantage and was willing to leave the inner workings mainly to others. He knew where his genius lay.

As he himself said: 'Don't let the noise of others drown out your inner voice.' Later in life, he explained it another way when referring to the band he preferred listening to above all others: 'My model for business is the Beatles. They were four guys who kept each other's kind of negative tendencies in check. They balanced each other, and the total was greater than the sum of the parts. That's how I see business: great things in business are never done by one person, they're done by a team of people.'

The second entrepreneurial rule is to turn defeat into victory by learning from your mistakes and revising your subsequent actions. The Apple II was followed by the launch of the Macintosh in 1984. After initial acclaim from the media and strong sales, demand slumped on account of its slow processing speed and narrow range of software. This led to an almighty feud within Apple. CEO John Sculley backed the open architecture of the Apple II, which made it popular with schools and small business. Jobs made the mistake of supporting the closed architecture of the Macintosh as a unique feature to compete against the IBM PC in the commercial market generally. It didn't work. Apple's fortunes waned, and in September 1985 Jobs resigned from the company he'd co-founded.

He did not lick his wounds for long. Along with several co-workers who'd left Apple with him, he started a new computer company called NeXT. In 1987, the company acquired the financial help of billionaire investor Henry Ross Perot, and the first NeXT workstations were rolled off the line in 1990. Jobs demonstrated his pursuit of aesthetic perfection by developing an exotic magnesium case for the product. He'd also expanded his interests in 1986, when he purchased an interest in Pixar, George Lucas's newly independent computer animation studio, and became its majority shareholder. Pixar's first film was the hugely successful *Toy Story* (1995), and many other hits followed. The studio went on to win twenty Academy Awards, nine Golden Globe Awards and eleven Grammy Awards.

Pixar was eventually sold to Disney for shares in 2006, and Jobs consequently became the biggest shareholder in Disney. Meanwhile, in 1997 he'd sold NeXT to his old company Apple and returned as de facto CEO, marking the beginning of a renaissance for the company with a wiser-for-the-experience Jobs at the helm.

As he recalled about his period outside Apple: 'The heaviness of being successful was replaced by the lightness of being a beginner again, less sure of everything. It freed me to enter one of the most creative periods of my life.' He had learnt from his mistake of overconfidence, which is what cost him his first career at Apple. We have on several occasions in this book mentioned that overconfidence is a vice to be avoided at all costs when thinking the future.

The third entrepreneurial rule is to be ahead of the market – by which we mean both producers and consumers alike – in identifying the next big thing, and then produce it as quickly as possible. While the Apple II offered many new features as a personal computer and was a smash hit, Jobs truly excelled in obeying this rule during his second stint at Apple.

With the release of iTunes and the iPod in 2001, the iPhone in 2007 and the iPad in 2010, Jobs ensured his place in history. In the same way that Henry Ford tweaked the design of a car so it could be mass-produced at an affordable price, or that Walt Disney reimagined the movie into an animated cartoon for both children and adults to enjoy, so Jobs revolutionised the Walkman into a device allowing thousands of songs to be downloaded from the internet.

Alongside other innovators, he transformed the classic mobile phone into a smartphone capable of multiple applications, and he redesigned the personal computer into a sleek object that could easily be carried around as an accessory. And he did it all before the average consumer was aware that it was time to move on to better things. His specific advice for this rule was: 'Get closer than ever to your customers. So close that you tell them what they need before they realize it themselves.'

As we said in Chapter 7, innovation goes hand in hand with adaptation. Jobs showed both qualities in adapting to life outside Apple for over ten years and then returning to Apple for the most innovative period of his career.

The fourth entrepreneurial rule is that innovation requires taking financial risks. Thus, you have to constantly play scenarios of how those risks might affect the solvency of the business. When the risks become too high, you must invite other investors to put capital into your business and spread the risks around. Starting out is always the toughest decision of all, particularly when you have little or no money. Wozniak sold his HP scientific calculator and Jobs his Volkswagen van to start Apple. It was no accident that Jobs selected his father's garage as the headquarters of the new company. However, there is another implication to this rule. You will be sacrificing time as well as money if you press 'go' and, because you only have one life, time can be more precious than money.

Apart from these four rules, Jobs did another thing superbly: he aligned his public image with the brands he was marketing. He came across as a minimalist who did not want to waste energy on anything outside of his goal to invent new products. He usually wore the same simple outfit of a black long-sleeved turtleneck, Levi's 501 classic-fit jeans and New Balance sneakers.

The unique, concentrated manner in which he described new products entranced his audiences. In his own way, he was like a nerdish movie star with loads of charisma and charm. Of course, this is not a necessary condition for being a successful entrepreneur; while you have to live and breathe the product or service and interact positively with all the essential players at the cornerstone of your business, you need not be a celebrity yourself. The pioneer does not always have to be in the public eye. Sometimes, though, it certainly helps.

Jobs often said that he wanted to put a ding in the universe. Both he and Mandela did it in their own ways. They were both ambitious people with goals of changing the big picture, and they worked out the minute details of walking the long road to achieve those goals. Thinking and doing came naturally to them. After all, you cannot influence that big circle beyond your control with thought alone. You have to convert your strategy into action in your own circle of control and in the sliver between the two circles. Then the sky is the limit.

As Mandela said: 'What counts in life is not the mere fact that we have lived. It is what difference we have made to the life of others that will determine the significance of the life we lead.' Jobs put it another way: 'Being the richest man in the cemetery doesn't matter to me. Going to bed at night saying we've done something wonderful, that's what matters to me.' Each made a difference in his own way using actions, not just words.

Now we need to do the same to save our planet. In 1976, it was revealed that chlorofluorocarbons (CFCs) were depleting the ozone layer in our atmosphere, which protects us from ultraviolet radiation. The latter can cause skin cancer and presents certain ecological issues. Shortly thereafter, the use of CFCs was banned in aerosol sprays and eventually in refrigeration and industrial cleaning. The latest evidence is that ozone depletion has slowed or stopped. So, together we *can* do it.

Abraham Lincoln said: 'The best thing about the future is that it comes one day at a time.' The way we interpret this is that the doing side can be incremental, with pauses for sleep, but in the long run the result can be life-changing. Not for nothing is a group of foxes sometimes called an earth!

As humble authors on a lower plane than the two giants of this chapter, we hope that we have put a ding in the universe of our readers to take the road to a better life. The dual purpose of our next, and final, chapter is to synthesise the wisdom of all the giants featured to make the ding as deep as possible, and to plant the seeds for a brighter future.

Now we come to this chapter's five questions, which will test how good you are at thinking *and* doing.

1. If we have managed to get you to do some scenario planning so far – or at least made you think about multiple ways the future can turn out – pick one best-case and one worst-case scenario that you've come up with. What five actions can you take towards making the ideal scenario a reality? And what five actions can help you avoid the worst one or protect you from its consequences if you can't stop it happening? Will you go ahead and take those actions?
2. When the future defies your expectations, either because of external factors or because your actions had unexpected consequences, do you automatically move to a Plan B, which you've already figured out by thinking flexibly about the future? Or do you start from scratch with a new plan? Maybe even cancel the project altogether?
3. Have there been times when you were rash because you were emotionally overwrought and put doing before thinking? What were the consequences? On the other hand, have there been times when you were too cautious and hesitant on the thinking side so that you missed the bus on the action side?
4. If you are not an entrepreneur, how would you convert our four entrepreneurial rules of thinking-then-doing into a form that gives you a good chance of winning the game that you are in?
5. What kind of ding have you put in the universe with your actions, and what do you intend to do now to make that ding wider and deeper? Do you reflect on the kind of legacy you want to leave when you depart from this world? Do you act accordingly?

Chapter 10

Planting Seeds

Knowledge is the only kind of wealth
that multiplies when you give it away.
Peter Schwartz

As an introduction to the final chapter, we think it is important to summarise the themes we've woven around the giants on whose shoulders we suggest you stand when thinking the future.

Isaiah Berlin – and Archilochus before him – offered us the metaphor of the hedgehog who knows one big thing and the fox who knows many things. We recommend that you be a fox in life in general and look at multiple possible futures in particular. It is safer than being a hedgehog betting on a single forecast.

Socrates made the case for going back to first principles and questioning all assumptions and assertions made on a topic under consideration. Working out what the future may have in store for us is an ideal subject for Socratic dialogue, either in one's own mind or with peers chosen for the diversity of their opinions. There are no ideas that should be treated as beyond criticism. The future is entirely open for debate.

The Stoic philosophers stressed that we should focus on the range of actions within our control in order to handle the challenges beyond our control. This is particularly important in tough situations. With this attitude, fear can be replaced by the determination to do the best we can in the circumstances, with the possibility of emerging stronger as a result of the experience.

Pierre Wack was one of the pioneers of scenario planning, which explores multiple possible futures as opposed to trying to predict the future in a single forecast. Scenario planning comes naturally to a fox, whereas forecasting is the domain of the hedgehog. To ensure that the scenarios are plausible, they are structured to accommodate the rules of the game, which apply to all scenarios, and to reflect the key uncertainties that will drive the future in one direction or another. Thus, because they form the foundations of the scenarios, the rules of the game and key uncertainties must be carefully selected in advance. The quote that opens this chapter comes from Peter Schwartz – widely regarded as America's top futurist. He succeeded Wack as head of scenario planning at Royal Dutch Shell and wrote the classic book on scenario planning: *The Art of the Long View: Planning for the Future in an Uncertain World.*

Karl Popper introduced a spectrum of predictability to indicate that our world's phenomena range from being highly unpredictable at one end, like the shape of a cloud, to fairly predictable at the other, like the workings of a clock. In thinking the future, we attach flags to scenarios to assess their probability as the future unfolds – from highly unlikely at one end of our spectrum to virtually certain at the other. Notably, it is often the highly unlikely scenario that can prove to be the most valuable to have in mind, because it has the potential to upend the status quo should it come to pass.

David Hume showed us the importance of an empirical approach – basing our knowledge solely on hard data obtained from experience. He also illuminated our tendency to indulge in wishful thinking, because reason is the slave of passion. Flags can offset this weakness, because they act as an antidote to emotion by helping us make objective judgments about which scenario is coming into play. Faith, on the other hand, gives us the will to do things. Trusting in yourself, and the spirit within, is more productive than trusting in the hand of fate. The uncertainty of the future makes the second option dicey, to say the least.

Charles Darwin concluded that the most successful species adapt to the changing natural environment, and that is why they outlive other species. We modified his theory by saying that because human beings have free will, they can innovate as well as adapt in charting the best course into the future.

Personal and institutional morality are central to any options for shaping our future, and Hannah Arendt, Philippa Foot, Martin Luther King Jr. and Dame Veronica Wedgwood drove this point home. We will inevitably face moral dilemmas in choosing how to act, and we will need to balance the short-term impact of our choices with their long-term consequences.

The paths we choose should not simply serve our own interests, but also abide by basic laws of morality. It is not all about power, glory and money.

Steve Jobs and Nelson Mandela both demonstrated how essential it is to convert futures thinking into action. That is where your reputation will stand or fall in the eyes of the people who follow you. Thinking obviously influences what we do but, vice versa, the experience of doing may alter what we have in mind to do next. They go hand in hand, and neither can function without the other.

In this final chapter, we hope to go full circle. This book has been about *thinking* the future more effectively; to end it off, we would like to look at where much of our thinking ability is shaped and developed: school.

The Seed of the Future

Until this point, the 'future' in this book's title has been presented as an expression of time. We now want to give it a human face. The year 2020 saw the arrival of the Covid-19 pandemic, which was not only one of the most significant events in recent memory, but a potential catalyst for change. Of particular interest to us is the opportunity to change education. Parents around the world are linked by a common concern: they want what's best for their children, and education is critical in that regard. It's the seed from which all else springs, and quite literally is the measure of our future.

In 2018, Mitch founded Growing Foxes, an education technology company focused on developing dynamic thinking in young people. In 2020 they hosted a two-week-long round-table discussion looking at the future of education. They brought together 140 key stakeholders in education, including school principals, teachers from a variety of subject areas, university professors, ministers of education, school pupils and leaders of industry. These participants came from six different countries: South Africa, Namibia, Uganda, the United Kingdom, Zambia and Zimbabwe. There was one overarching question: What will education look like in 2030? Such a broad and daunting question could have been overwhelming, so the Growing Foxes team broke it down into parts, structured around a methodology, to guide the conversation. They facilitated the engagement throughout to ensure that the discussion was robust but focused. Various discussion topics then branched out of each step of the methodology to allow the participants to raise and explore important points relevant to the overall strategic question.

They used the opportunity presented by the coronavirus pandemic to facilitate the discussion virtually, not only to abide by social-distancing regulations, but also to *live* what many innovators in education have been pointing to as the future – a blended approach to peer-to-peer engagement that incorporates the use of technology. Accordingly, instead of simply holding the conversation online in a two-hour Zoom call, the discussion was facilitated over two weeks through a web-based platform designed by Growing Foxes. This not only allowed participants time to reflect on their engagement and the engagement of others, it also mitigated what facilitators so often see in time-pressured strategy sessions – some individuals dominating the discussion, leaving little time for others to contribute.

The discussion started with a frank contextual assessment of the current reality of education. This process encapsulated the fundamental contradiction that would emerge throughout the overall discussion, and which lies at the heart of education: incredibly passionate individuals have become increasingly frustrated at the inflexibility of a system that resists change. There was wide agreement that school-based education is stuck in the past, tied to a legacy model designed in a bygone age.

Although there are pockets of excellence, inequality is rife, and the discussions revealed this to be as true for the United Kingdom as it is for Uganda. Ultimately this translates into further disparities as learners progress from school or drop out altogether. Subjects are taught in silos, with little to no interdisciplinary focus, contrasting sharply with the way professional work is evolving.

Assessment is exam-driven, narrowing the scope for curious and challenging minds to grow. Put simply, the common concern among *all* participants was that the current system is unfit to develop young minds so that they are prepared for a rapidly changing new world of work, and the ever-increasing role that technology will play in their lives.

This contextual discussion was a stark reminder of the enormity of the challenge facing education. But the contextual grounding also allowed the participants to articulate more clearly what they believe to be the rules of the game – the relatively fixed patterns they're confident will persist no matter what scenario materialises. This was crucial, as it injected some clarity into an otherwise hazy picture.

One of the fundamental rules the participants pointed to was that a country's economic success will always be linked to the quality of its education system. The rule stands firm under Socratic scrutiny: a country's economic competitiveness is dictated by the quality of its citizens' skills, and the quality of these skills is shaped by the country's educational make-up. Some skills may be developed in other countries when individuals study abroad and then return, but only a fraction of the overall population is able to do so. The logic of this rule is sound, and hence we are confident that it is a reliable assumption for all possible futures.

Another rule of the game is that teachers will always be needed. Despite the rapid advancement of technology, no artificial intelligence has yet been able to capture the magic of human-led facilitation. We should never take this for granted. We, as humans, have an innate ability to teach each other – to guide learning, prompt curiosity and provoke stimulating debate. However, it's important to point out that this rule will only persist up to the horizon of the discussion's strategic scope: 2030.

Beyond that, the role, function and relevance of teachers will morph into a key uncertainty. Technology may catch up with our uniquely human ability to facilitate knowledge sharing, and teachers may be supplanted with digital counterparts that are cheaper, more powerful, more efficient and less unionised. The foxy decision-makers leading education institutions should have twitching ears and wiggling whiskers at this point. With robust and innovative teacher training, they can safeguard, or at least extend, the human quotient in education. This is within their circle of control.

One unnerving rule emerged from the session: central *physical* spaces for learning will become less important. We have already seen this trend over the last few years with the advent of sophisticated learning platforms, and the abundance of available digital educational content. With an entry-level technological device and a stable internet connection, any learner can access a vast wealth of information and receive guided skills development in almost any domain of human ingenuity. The world is literally at their fingertips.

This means that a physical space where learners congregate for synchronous, face-to-face lessons is becoming increasingly anachronistic. Not only are such spaces not needed to facilitate a productive learning experience, but the large overheads that come with them only serve to increase the cost of education. The digital, technology-led option, which has always been seen as too expensive to implement for schools of humble means, is fast approaching a tipping point where it becomes the much cheaper option. Indeed, many advances have already reached this point, and with growing scale, the costs of technology are only going to decrease further.

Think of the costs and logistics involved in owning a sizeable amount of land, building and maintaining brick-and-mortar structures to house learners, servicing those properties with water and electricity, transporting all the relevant parties to this one place, and printing and reprinting textbooks every year. Compare that with one device and an internet connection, where new innovations, new content and a world of information can be beamed into one's hands and eyes in an instant. The logic of this rule is sound and, if nothing else, the coronavirus pandemic has proved to be a compulsory and experimental assessment of its viability.

We should not, however, take on this rule without serious scrutiny. A Socratic challenger may highlight the need for physical spaces for social interaction, spontaneous conversation, and cultural and sporting activities – all important facets of well-rounded development. A future without such physical interaction would undoubtedly be a poorer one and would not only leave learners yearning for more human contact, but also make them more socially awkward and less versatile.

Then again, who is to say that a child's social and physical interactions need to take place at a central academic location? Learners can also gather at various sporting and cultural clubs outside of school to complement their academic studies. We just need to reimagine our current conception of what school *is* to see what it *could be*. The challenge of complying with this rule that schools on a single site will be phased out is not beyond the reach of the average community. A school can be physically decentralised into a suite of platforms that combine in an effective way to produce an overall learning experience in step with modern times.

There is one final rule of the game to take into account: parents will always have to work, and so there will always be a need to outsource education. Although some parents have the capacity to home-school their children, this is not possible for everybody. Work takes time and attention, and so parents rely on the services of educational institutions, whether they be private businesses or state facilities. Hence, the demand for education-focused entities will remain a constant.

Those parents who juggled caring for bored and antsy children while working from home during the months of Covid-19 lockdown would probably attest to this. In turn, this rule of the game means that parents will always have to weigh up where to have their children schooled, or at least how they will be educated. This puts emphasis on trust and the reputation of the education entities involved, as well as the real-life results they can promise to a prospective parent.

If these are some of the rules of the game for education, what then are the key uncertainties? The participants in the Growing Foxes education round table highlighted many but, broadly speaking, most of them could be grouped into two crucial categories: how education links to the world in which it operates, which was defined as the *relevance of education*; and the mindset of the people who do the educating, which was summed up as the *culture of openness or resistance to change* among educators and relevant players. Plotted on a set of axes, these two critical uncertainties produced four potential scenarios. As you explore them, reflect on where you believe your country's education system currently sits, and where you think it is heading.

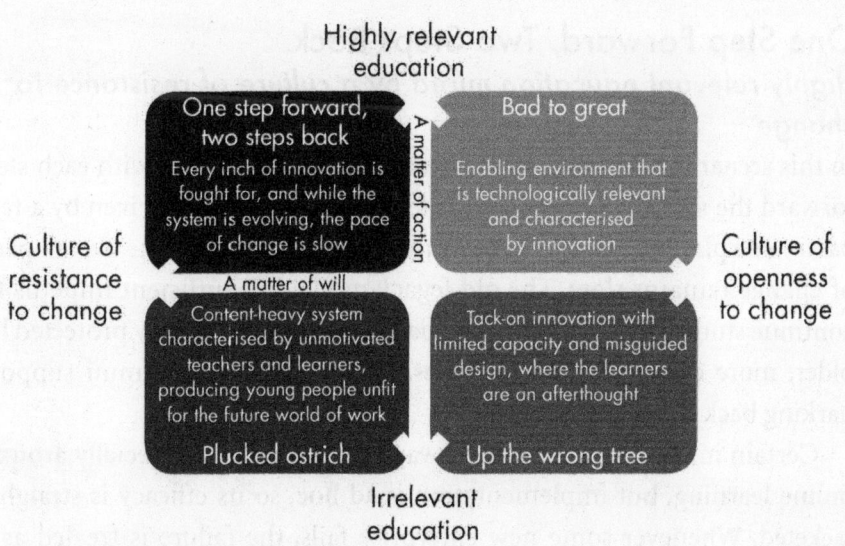

Bad to Great
Highly relevant education supported by a culture of openness to change

This scenario is characterised by innovation and an enabling educational environment that is technologically relevant. The system becomes far more flexible and dynamic, constantly evolving with the changing world of work to develop in students the necessary skills to flourish. 'Subjects' become a thing of the past and are replaced with a much more interdisciplinary curriculum incorporating a wider, more nuanced perspective of our integrated world. Students are encouraged to think critically and their curiosity is rewarded. They are empowered to shape their learning, set their own direction and have greater responsibility over their future. Soft skills and communication are prioritised to ensure a more ethical society, and students are taught proficiencies in areas where artificial intelligence and machine learning can't compete yet. Teacher training is done regularly and with enthusiasm because, in this scenario, an overall culture of openness to change supports all upskilling efforts. A more relevant education system translates into more successful and entrepreneurially driven national economies. These, in turn, lead the state to deliver greater budgetary support for the further development of schools. Overall, education moves in the direction from bad to great.

One Step Forward, Two Steps Back
Highly relevant education mired by a culture of resistance to change

In this scenario, every inch of innovation is fought for, but with each step forward the system is pushed two steps back. Progress is driven by a few passionate players, but they're swimming against the tide. The overall pace of change remains slow. The old legacy model has sufficient impetus to continue stumbling on, and out-of-date traditions are closely protected by older, more conservative authorities, backed by strong alumni support harking back to the days of old.

Certain innovations force their way into the system, especially around online learning, but implementation is ad hoc, so its efficacy is straight-jacketed. Whenever some new enterprise fails, the failure is treated as a reason to maintain the status quo. A few schools manage to transition to a more relevant education model and curriculum content, but they remain stifled by the broader educational environment configured by top-down state regulations. Furthermore, the uneven pace of change worsens inequality between schools.

Up the Wrong Tree
A culture of openness to change causes education to become increasingly irrelevant

There is a fundamental shift in the culture of openness to change within the education system, but the initiatives taken to change it are misguided. The coronavirus pandemic accelerates the shift to incorporate technology, but the speed of the shift doesn't allow enough time for curriculum designers to pair fresh content and revised pedagogy with the new mediums of learning. Teachers and principals pat themselves on the back for bringing in innovation, but students are left worse off as they struggle with the transition and fail to have a more enriched learning experience. As a result, the learning outcomes for students do not substantially improve.

Budgetary constraints mean that although there is a flurry of ideas around what should change, a lack of resources constrains the action taken to support those ideas. The private sector gets more involved but lacks a strategic understanding of the demands of education, so it puts funding and emphasis in the wrong places. Although the increased use of technology generates more and more data, schools fail to incorporate that data wisely.

Teachers are passionate and eager to develop their skills, but the pace of change and the misalignment between pedagogy and technological innovation make it difficult for them to implement the new teaching methods. Fourth-industrial-revolution subjects, such as coding and robotics, are tacked on to an already overloaded curriculum, and governments fail to train specialist teachers to teach them. The system is set on a new path with so much momentum that it is difficult to pause and rethink its development. Despite a growing culture of openness to change, attempts at innovation are barking up the wrong tree.

Plucked Ostrich
A culture of resistance to change entrenches increasingly irrelevant education

In this worst-case scenario, most of the decision-makers in education stick their heads in the sand. They are either oblivious to the need for change or are aware but refuse to do anything about it. Increasingly weary, over-worked and underpaid teachers lose enthusiasm and feel truly plucked. Students reflect the apathy of their teachers and lack the motivation to learn or the aspiration to improve themselves. This is made worse by content-heavy subjects that sit in silos. The students feel like cogs in a big and complex machine designed to churn them out, not nurture them. They have no responsibility and are punished with outdated methods of discipline if they step out of line.

There are few attempts to revise the curriculum, and those that do exist find little favour, meaning there is a growing gap between what is being taught and what students have to deal with in the world beyond school. Businesses become increasingly alarmed at the quality of students they can recruit and have to play a more meaningful role in training and upskilling to ensure that employees meet job requirements. The failures in the education system translate into greater youth unemployment, social unrest, lack of innovation and low levels of entrepreneurial spirit in society. Because the system is so entrenched and cumbersome, it is incredibly difficult to influence or change in any meaningful way. Thus, the status quo is likely to persist for decades to come.

What should strike you when reading through each of the above scenarios is just how essential education is for the prospects of a given country and, more importantly, the future of humanity. It's the combination of soil, water, sun and air that either nurtures or destroys the potential of seedlings to grow into full bloom and then feed back into the national and global ecosystem. Education marks the most crucial flag to watch when thinking the future. For us, it is the number-one determinant for the success of a 'winning nation'. This why we believe it is important to reflect on the future of education to end this book.

Based on the critical uncertainties driving our four education scenarios, we have identified five flags that parents, parents-to-be, grandparents and future-employers can watch to assess the direction in which their education system is heading. The first, and perhaps most significant, flag, is the flexibility of government regulation around education. Round-table participants argued that the main choking point of the current system is the rigid reliance on final examinations.

Effectively, much of secondary education is geared towards meeting state-stipulated requirements for final assessments. While a common nation-wide assessment has its benefits, the inflexibility of the assessment model means that innovation is stifled in the name of meeting certain prerequisites. Not only do these remain largely unchanged for years, but they also force all teaching, and therefore all students, into a fixed mould, designed to fit the median without exploring the novel and unusual.

Governments will need to allow for greater regulatory flexibility without compromising on quality and merit. If they get it right, this will be a major flag for unleashing more long-lasting innovation in education. This is the most important flag to have on your radar, as all schools must play within the rules of the game set by their national regulatory framework.

The second flag to watch is a possible shift towards a more interdisciplinary approach in the curricula. Many subjects currently sit in silos. They're delivered by subject specialists within neatly defined bounds of what constitutes a 'subject'. But life isn't neatly divided in this way. Politics, economics, sociology, technology and the environment are all intertwined, and change in one area can reverberate across the interconnected system. If education is to move from where it is to where it should be, as scripted in the Bad to Great scenario, it will have to become more relevant, and the first step on that path is to weave subjects together to provide a more holistic approach.

Learners with an interest in science need to know how science affects humans, and so they need to be schooled in the arts and humanities; they ought to understand the *context* in which science is carried out. Similarly, those learners who favour drama, art and languages need to understand how science and technology will play pivotal roles in their lives. There are schools moving towards a more integrated approach to education, and the general *culture of openness to change* will be a key factor in determining which schools move faster than others in developing youthful foxiness by introducing more relevant and interdisciplinary curricula.

A third flag to have on your radar is the quality of teacher training, selection and remuneration. Countries that pay teachers well get the best candidates. In terms of selection, there are schools that have cottoned on to the idea that young learners are more likely to relate to younger teachers. While lacking the experience of their senior counterparts, younger teachers are often more dynamic and flexible in their approach, and some schools therefore make a priority of seeking the right age composition for their staff. However, this is no silver bullet.

To deliver a truly relevant and insightful teaching experience, governments, universities and schools will have to continually update their teacher-training models. Teachers will need to know how to integrate subjects that facilitate probing discussions between learners and encourage them to entertain different perspectives. They will also need to know how to effectively integrate the use of technology into lessons. This is something that school heads can manage. Expect this flag to be one of the first to rise if the system evolves in the right direction – it will be the one that creates the most positive impact on learners.

The precursor to the above flag is the dynamism of school principals, and this is the fourth flag you should have on your radar. It is the one that will enable you to assess the quality of education at a more *granular* level – such as parents deciding where to send their children to school. Principals are very much the gatekeepers of education, especially secondary education. They're the captains who steer the school ship, and like CEOs in business, they ultimately either drive or inhibit innovation within their organisation. Experience works both ways in the top job: it can be a source of effective adaptation, or it can be an impediment to change.

Hence, there are several key questions in tracking this flag. Will there be enough existing principals who are keen to adopt the new models in the Bad to Great scenario? How many will stick to a 'don't rock the boat' approach to education strategy? When hiring principals and other departmental heads, will an emphasis be put on recruiting new blood into the corps of senior leadership? Are decision-makers identifying those adventurous teachers with a greater understanding of the shifting coalface? More controversially, will the powers that be bring in people from outside education altogether to shake up the status quo? Time alone will deliver the answers.

Finally, one more flag to watch is the evolving architecture on school grounds. Traditionally, the sign of a functioning school is a big hall for assembly and various blocks of classrooms furnished with desks and either a chalkboard or whiteboard. More privileged schools feature a swimming pool and sports fields. These have been considered necessary and sufficient fixtures, but in line with the above rules of the game, their place in education is coming under scrutiny. The coronavirus pandemic showed that it wasn't necessary for everyone to assemble in a physical space each day. Nor was it necessary to conduct class in a class*room*.

In addition, chalkboards and whiteboards just don't cut it any more. For learners, the contrast between watching the latest *Avengers* movie on the weekend, with a production budget of hundreds of millions of dollars, and a teacher standing at the front of a room, chalk in hand, is staggering. How can so much money and organisation go into *entertaining* young people, and not even a fraction of that go into *educating* them?

Going forward, capturing learners' attention will require far greater creativity, money, effort and production value, the likes of which are simply impossible with squiggles of chalk or whiteboard marker. Progress is also inconceivable when the majority of schools continue to assume that they are the *sole* generators of content. They will have to be more imaginative in how they can instead act as *aggregators* of relevant material produced by creators beyond school. This material is often either free or very cheap. Moreover, if they want to attract and maintain learners in a *physical* space, schools will have to give careful thought to their unique selling points. They will need media centres and high-speed, stable internet connections, in addition to spaces for social interaction that the virtual world simply can't replicate. Watch this flag to assess if education is heading towards Bad to Great, or the way of a Plucked Ostrich.

Taking into consideration all of the above, our advice to leaders in the field of education would be to return to first principles, then decide how to evolve from there. We would pose the following Socratic question: If you could develop one core skill in young people today to set them up well for life, what would it be? Our answer: Effectively thinking the future to make better decisions in an uncertain and ever-changing world.

This core skill is central to so many aspects of all our lives: planning for yourself, your family or your business, engaging with others, navigating relationships, choosing where to invest your time and money and, of course, chasing your dreams – when you're young *and* when you're old. Effective futures thinking can play a role in every decision you make and is critical to successfully managing these different dimensions to your life.

Hopefully our readers who are involved in education will be able to take something away from this advice and start creating the next generation of foxes. And those who are not involved in education but are nevertheless impacted by it (which is all of us) will have a scenario framework through which they can assess how the future may play out. But let's now broaden our scope beyond education and return to summing up the principles of this book.

Was our purpose to change the way the world's leaders think the future? Was it to overturn centuries of deterministic thinking? Was it to revolutionise the way the future is taught at the top business schools? No, our motivation was a little more modest: to look back at some of history's greatest thinkers and distil a set of principles that you, the reader, can embody to think the future more effectively – for both the big and small decisions in your life. It is up to you to judge us on whether we have succeeded or not.

Conclusion

It is wrong to believe that futures thinking has a defined outcome, like the single prediction of a forecaster made at a specific point in time. Rather, it is an *ongoing activity* because the future is forever unfolding before us, and we should never be so conceited as to think we have captured it fully. There is no termination point, which means there is always thinking to be done. Hopefully, by incorporating the principles of this book, you will be able to perform the activity with the excellence it deserves.

The ancient Greeks had a word for such excellence: *areté*. It wasn't something to be achieved in a single act. Aristotle defined it as the continual application of good habits over time. By fleshing out the ideas of the giants we chose, we want to turn you into a habitual fox who looks at the future from different angles, who readily adapts to whatever the future brings, and who is agile and innovative when turning thoughts into action.

We don't want you to feel that you need to become a giant yourself to lead a fulfilling life. Foxes are stoical characters who make the best out of what they've been given. You can't control the circumstances of your birth, but you have some control over what you do thereafter, for however long you live. Thinking the future in a rational way along the lines we have suggested should give you a head-start in making your own footprint in the world. May the fox be with you in doing so.

We would like to end this final chapter with just one question about the *process* of thinking the future:

What, for you, are the key takeaways from this book that will change the way you think the future from now on?

A Final Spartan Reminder

We have all along challenged the conventional motivational message that if you firmly set your goals and pursue them, you will define your future. This message, in and of itself, is not necessarily a bad thing. But it invites hubris, and hubris can lead to nemesis, which jeopardises everything you may have hoped for. Here's one last story to drive that point home.

Flush with victory after invading a number of city-states in southern Greece, King Phillip of Macedon, father of the famous Alexander the Great, turned his attention to the powerful Sparta. He besieged the city and, confident of the outcome, sent an unambiguous threat to its leaders:

'If I defeat you, we will raze your city to the ground. We will kill every man and boy in the city and take every woman and girl into slavery.' The Spartans sent a one-word reply: '*If*...'

Bibliography

Alberge, Dalya. '"Deaf" genius Beethoven was able to hear his final symphony after all', *Guardian*, 1 February 2020. https://www.theguardian.com/music/2020/feb/01/beethoven-not-completely-deaf-says-musicologist [last accessed April 2021]

Arendt, Hannah. *Eichmann in Jerusalem*. New York: Viking Press, 1963

———. *The Human Condition*. University of Chicago Press, 1958

———. *The Origins of Totalitarianism*. New York: Schocken Books, 1951

Baggini, Julian, and Simon Jenkins. 'Is reason the slave of the passions?', *Prospect*, 4 May 2019. https://www.prospectmagazine.co.uk/magazine/is-reason-the-slave-of-the-passions-philosophy-hume [last accessed April 2021]

Berlin, Isaiah. *The Hedgehog and The Fox: An Essay on Tolstoy's View of History*. Princeton University Press, 2013

———. 'Notes on Prejudice', *New York Review of Books*, 18 October 2001. https://www.nybooks.com/articles/2001/10/18/notes-on-prejudice/ [last accessed April 2021]

Butler, Judith. 'Hannah Arendt's challenge to Adolf Eichmann', *Guardian*, 29 August 2011. https://www.theguardian.com/commentisfree/2011/aug/29/hannah-arendt-adolf-eichmann-banality-of-evil [last accessed April 2021]

Cameron, David. 'David Cameron speech: UK and the EU', *BBC News*, 23 January 2013. https://www.bbc.com/news/uk-politics-21158316 [last accessed April 2021]

———. 'Text of David Cameron's speech after "Brexit" vote', *New York Times*, 25 June 2016. https://www.nytimes.com/2016/06/25/world/europe/david-cameron-speech-transcript.html [last accessed April 2021]

Cieplak-Mayr von Baldegg, Kasia. 'Time capsule: An hour with Steve Jobs in 1990', *Atlantic*, 11 October 2011. https://www.theatlantic.com/technology/archive/2011/10/time-capsule-an-hour-with-steve-jobs-in-1990/246388/ [last accessed April 2021]

Collins, Jim. *Good to Great: Why Some Companies Make the Leap ... and Others Don't*. New York: Harper Business, 2001

Critchley, Simon. *Tragedy, the Greeks, and Us*. New York: Pantheon Books, 2019

Darwin, Charles. *On the Origin of Species*. London: Macmillan Collector's Library, 2017

Del Rey, Jason. 'This is the Jeff Bezos playbook for preventing Amazon's demise', *Vox*, 12 April 2017. https://www.vox.com/2017/4/12/15274220/jeff-bezos-amazon-shareholders-letter-day-2-disagree-and-commit [last accessed April 2021]

de Soto, Hernando. *The Mystery of Capital: Why Capitalism Triumphs in the West and Fails Everywhere Else*. New York: Basic Books, 2000

de Tocqueville, Alexis. 'Introductory Chapter' in *Democracy in America*, Henry Reeve (tr.). Project Gutenberg. https://www.marxists.org/reference/archive/de-tocqueville/democracy-america/ch00.htm [last accessed April 2021]

Drucker, Peter. *The Practice of Management*. New York: Harper Business, 1954

Durant, Will. *The Story of Philosophy: The Lives and Opinions of the Great Philosophers of the Western World*. New York: Simon and Schuster, 1961

'Emissions Gap Report', UNEP, 9 December 2020. https://www.unep.org/emissions-gap-report-2020 [last accessed April 2021]

Farber, Dan. 'Tim Cook maintains Steve Jobs' Beatles business model', *CNET*, 12 June 2013. https://www.cnet.com/news/tim-cook-maintains-steve-jobs-beatles-business-model/ [last accessed April 2021]

Feynman, Richard P. 'The Uncertainty of Science', *New York Times*. https://archive.nytimes.com/www.nytimes.com/books/first/f/feynman-meaning.html [last accessed April 2021]

Fifield, Anna. 'New Zealand isn't just flattening the curve. It's squashing it.' *The Washington Post*, April 7, 2020

Forde, Dana. 'Mandela's life inspires service community', Nelson Mandela Foundation, 22 July 2014. https://www.nelsonmandela.org/news/entry/mandelas-life-inspires-service-community [last accessed April 2021]

Fry, Stephen. *Troy*. London: Penguin Michael Joseph, 2020

Gareth Price's Symposium (Shell Group Planning, 1994)

Grant, Adam. *Originals: How Non-conformists Change the World*. London: WH Allen, 2016

Gray, Louise. 'David Attenborough – humans are plague on Earth', *Telegraph*, 22 January 2013. https://www.telegraph.co.uk/news/earth/earthnews/9815862/Humans-are-plague-on-Earth-Attenborough.html [last accessed April 2021]

Herschel, John Frederick William. *Preliminary Discourse on the Study of Natural Philosophy*. Cambridge: Cambridge University Press, 2009

Holiday, Ryan, and Stephen Hanselman. *The Daily Stoic: 366 Meditations on Wisdom, Perseverance, and the Art of Living*. New York: Portfolio, 2016

Hughes, Thomas L. 'The Fate of Facts in the World of Men', Proceedings of the

American Society of International Law at Its Annual Meeting (1921–1969), Vol. 63, 1969, pp. 233–245. https://www.jstor.org/stable/25657791 [last accessed April 2021]

Hume, David. *An Enquiry Concerning Human Understanding*, P.F. Millican (ed.). Oxford University Press, 2007

———. *A Treatise of Human Nature*, David F. Norton and Mary J. Norton (eds.). Oxford University Press, 2000

Ilbury, Chantell, and Clem Sunter. *The Mind of a Fox*. Cape Town: Human & Rousseau, 1999

Jacobs, Alan. *Breaking Bread with the Dead: A Reader's Guide to a More Tranquil Mind*. London: Penguin Press, 2020

Jobs, Steve. 'Steve Jobs 2005 Stanford commencement address.' Farnham Street, July 2014. https://fs.blog/2014/07/steve-jobs-stanford-commencement/ [last accessed April 2021]

Kahn, Herman. *On Thermonuclear War*. New Jersey: Princeton University Press, 1960

Kelly, Jemima. 'In uncertain times, certainty is over-rated and over-rewarded', *Financial Times*, 14 January 2021. https://www.ft.com/content/f4ab5665-b6fc-4cc6-92e7-8bd13d6b9d46 [last accessed April 2021]

King, Martin Luther, Jr. '"I have a dream" speech, in its entirety', *NPR*, 18 June 2010. https://www.npr.org/2010/01/18/122701268/i-have-a-dream-speech-in-its-entirety [last accessed April 2021]

Leavitt, Michael. 'Computer Simulation in International Relations Forecasting,' in Choucri, N. and Robinson, T.W. (eds.) *Forecasting in International Relations: Theory, Methods, Problems, Prospects*. San Francisco: Freeman, 1978

'"Let's have trial by combat" over election – Giuliani', Reuters, 6 January 2021. https://www.reuters.com/video/watch/idOVDU2NS9R [last accessed April 2021]

Mandela, Nelson. *Long Walk to Freedom*. New York: Little, Brown, 1994

Nagel, Thomas. 'What We Owe a Rabbit', *New York Review of Books*, 21 March 2019. https://www.nybooks.com/articles/2019/03/21/christine-korsgaard-what-we-owe-a-rabbit/ [last accessed April 2021]

Oliver, Craig. *Unleashing Demons: The Inside Story of Brexit*. London: Hodder & Stoughton, 2016

Oppenheimer, Michael. *Pivotal Countries, Alternate Futures: Using Scenarios to Manage American Strategy*. New York: Oxford University Press, 2016

Popper, Karl. *The Logic of Scientific Discovery*. London: Routledge, 2002

———. *Of Clouds and Clocks: An Approach to the Problem of Rationality and the Freedom of Man*. St. Louis: Washington University, 1966

Rasmussen, Dennis C. *The Infidel and the Professor: David Hume, Adam Smith, and the Friendship That Shaped Modern Thought*. Princeton University Press, 2017

Sewall, Richard B. *The Vision of Tragedy*. New Haven: Yale University Press, 1959

'So if Beethoven was completely deaf, how did he compose?', *Classic FM*, 3 September 2020. https://www.classicfm.com/composers/beethoven/guides/deaf-hearing-loss-composing/ [last accessed April 2021]

Sunter, Clem. *Never Mind the Millennium. What about the next 24 hours?* Cape Town: Human & Rousseau, 1999

———. *The World and South Africa in the 1990s*. Cape Town: Human & Rousseau, 1987

Sun Tzu. *The Art of War*, Samuel B. Griffith (tr.). Oxford: Clarendon Press, 1964

Tetlock, Philip. *Expert Political Judgement: How Good Is It? How Can We Know?* Princeton University Press, 2005

'Time to care: Unpaid and underpaid care work and the global inequality crisis', Oxfam International, 20 January 2020. https://www.oxfam.org/en/research/time-care [last accessed April 2021]

Vernant, Jean-Pierre, and Pierre Vidal-Naquet. *Myth and Tragedy in Ancient Greece*. Translated by Janet Lloyd. New Jersey: Princeton University Press, 1990.

Wack, Pierre. 'Scenarios: Uncharted waters ahead', *Harvard Business Review*, September 1985. https://hbr.org/1985/09/scenarios-uncharted-waters-ahead [last accessed April 2021]

———. 'Scenarios: Shooting the Rapids' *Harvard Business Review*, September 1985. https://hbr.org/1985/11/scenarios-shooting-the-rapids [last accessed April 2021]

Wedgwood, C.V. *The King's War, 1641–1647*. London: Collins, 1958

———. *History and Hope: The Collected Essays of C.V. Wedgwood*. London: Fontana, 1987

Weil, Herman, and Michael Leavitt. 'Dynamic Modeling of Central Environmental Descriptors for Eastern and Western Europe', National Technical Information Service, United States Department of Commerce, 1973

Wells, Herbert George. *The Time Machine*. London: Penguin Random House, 2010

Wittenberg, Steven Gregg. 'Churchill Appraises Hitler', BA thesis, University of Illinois, 1992. https://www.ideals.illinois.edu/bitstream/handle/2142/93994/30112111736770_opt.pdf?sequence=1 [last accessed April 2021]

Wohlstetter, Roberta. *Pearl Harbor: Warning and Decision*. Stanford University Press, 1962